Albert
the Great:

The Albert Pujols Story

ROB RAINS

www.SportsPublishingLLC.com

ISBN: 1-58261-892-5

Publishers: Peter L. Bannon and Joseph J. Bannon Sr.
Senior managing editor: Susan M. Moyer
Acquisitions editor: Mike Pearson
Developmental editor: Doug Hoepker
Art director: K. Jeffrey Higgerson
Book design: Heidi Norsen
Dust jacket design: Dustin Hubbart
Project manager: Heidi Norsen
Imaging: Dustin Hubbart, Heidi Norsen, Kenneth O'Brien
Photo editor: Erin Linden-Levy
Vice president of sales and marketing: Kevin King
Media and promotions managers: Mike Hagan (regional),
        Randy Fouts (national), Maurey Williamson (print)

Printed in Hong Kong

Sports Publishing L.L.C.
804 North Neil Street
Champaign, IL 61820

Phone: 1-877-424-2665
Fax: 217-363-2073
Web site: www.SportsPublishingLLC.com

To all the young
        Cardinal fans who
hope one day to be
        "the next Albert Pujols."

Table of Contents

Chapter 1
Introducing Albert the Great   2

Chapter 2
A Young Albert   8

Chapter 3
Learning the Language and Baseball   12

Chapter 4
A Minor Leaguer   20

Chapter 5
Making the Cut   28

Chapter 6
Rookie of the Year   34

Chapter 7
Building on Success   50

Chapter 8
A Banner Season   66

Chapter 9
A Trip to the Series   76

Chapter 10
Faith and Family   86

Chapter 11
How Good Can He Be?   94

Career Stats   114

Career Home Runs   115

Milestones   118

Introducing Albert The Great

In just four short seasons at the major league level, Albert Pujols already has established a legacy that will endure for years. No player, including Hall of Famers Ted Williams and Joe DiMaggio, has ever burst onto the scene the way the young native of the Dominican Republic has since arriving in St. Louis at the start of the 2001 season.

An unknown 13th-round draft pick from a small junior college, Albert had played only a handful of games above the low Class A level when he made the Cardinals' starting lineup as a 21-year-old rookie. During that first spring training, observers could not believe what they were witnessing. How could this young, untested player be so good? Those questions remained throughout Albert's first season, which he capped off by becoming the ninth unanimous Rookie of the Year in National League history. Skeptics wondered if he would be a one-year wonder. Albert responded to that with a resounding

ROBERT LABERGE/GETTY IMAGES

Albert the Great: The Albert Pujols Story

Did you know...?

In the first four seasons of his career Albert has drawn 304 walks and struck out only 279 times in 2,728 plate appearances.

LEFT: Teammates and opponents agree that one of the reasons for Albert's success is his intense focus on the game.

second season that saw him finish as the runner up to Barry Bonds for the N.L. MVP award.

He has gone on to establish himself as one of the leading hitters in baseball, regardless of age, and earn his place next to the Yankees' Alex Rodriguez as one of the game's biggest stars to watch over the next decade. Already considered by most observers to be the best Cardinals player since Stan Musial, Albert is on a pace to rewrite the team's record book if he continues to perform at such a high level for the next decade.

"If he stays healthy and keeps performing like he's performing, which you expect, he's going to keep breaking records and do things that nobody's done before," said former Cardinal and current broadcaster Mike Shannon.

Added Cardinals manager Tony La Russa, "[With] talent like that and a

"[With] talent like

that and a willingness

to compete, he's

capable of doing

(T O N Y L A R U S S A)

anything."

RIGHT: Albert is congratulated by teammates after his game-winning home run in the 10th inning defeated the Cincinnati Reds on June 18, 2004.

willingness to compete, he's capable of doing anything."

His performance in the 2004 postseason showed that Albert is capable of rising to challenges, helping the Cardinals beat the Los Angeles Dodgers in the first round, then earning MVP honors as St. Louis beat Houston in seven games to capture its first pennant in 17 years. He was the Cardinals' lone productive hitter in the middle of the lineup in the four-game loss to the Boston Red Sox in the World Series. Albert kept his head high when the Series was over, vowing that he, and the team, would be back on this national stage in the near future and that the next time, the result would be different.

There is no reason to doubt him.

Combining his on-field performance with his off-field character and support of charitable causes, Albert has proven that he is worthy of being one of the leading citizens of Cardinal Nation.

AP/WWP

Albert the Great: The Albert Pujols Story

A Young Albert

CHAPTER TWO

Jose Albert Pujols might not have been born to play baseball, but he definitely had baseball in his blood.

Albert's father, Bienvenido, was a pitcher and was known throughout his native Dominican Republic. He was often away from home, looking for work, leaving Albert and his brothers and sisters to be raised by their grandmother, America. America had 11 children, including Bienvenido, and many of Albert's aunts and uncles also lived at the family home and were more like brothers and sisters to him.

Albert was born on January 16, 1980, in Santo Domingo. His family was poor and often survived on government assistance. Despite the financial hardships, his grandmother made certain Albert had a happy childhood. From the age of six, the youngster could be found outside, on the dusty fields near his home, playing with sticks and balls. He recalls often playing catch with a lime, and fashioning gloves out of cardboard milk cartons. A stick could always be found for use as a bat.

When Albert received the chance, he tagged along with his father to one of his games. Whenever he wasn't playing baseball or watching his father play, Albert was watching whatever games were on television. Usually it was the Atlanta Braves, but he never had a particular favorite team or player as he was growing up. Most of his attention was focused on the Latin players, including Sammy Sosa, Raul Mondesi and others. He also was interested in the history of the game and learning about other Latin American stars such as Roberto Clemente, Tony Perez and Juan Marichal.

As he grew, his baseball talent began to emerge. By the time he was a teenager, he had displayed enough skills to begin earning attention from scouts, who issued him invitations to baseball camps sponsored by some of the major league clubs. Albert was one of the many young Dominicans who viewed baseball as the opportunity to provide his family with a better life.

Despite having enough ability to get invited to the camps, the young Albert did not show enough promise for either the Florida Marlins or Oakland A's to sign him to a minor league contract when he attended their camps as a 16-year-old. He was disappointed but was determined not to give up on his dream of making it to the major leagues.

By that time, several members of the Pujols family had moved to New York, and America decided the rest of the family should move there as well. Bienvenido and

Did you know...?

Albert's father, Bienvenido, was a pitcher in his native Dominican Republic. A young Albert would occasionally accompany his father to games.

Albert were included, and they left the Dominican Republic for New York in the summer of 1996.

Their stay in New York was brief. The city turned out to be too expensive and violent, and America did not think it was a good place to raise her grandson. One day, he was running an errand for his grandmother to buy groceries. While on the errand, he witnessed a shooting—only a few feet away from where he was standing. When he got home and told America what had happened, she made the decision to move the family once again.

Some of the family members heard that there was a town in the Midwest where about 2,000 Dominican immigrants had settled. That was good enough information for America, so she, her son and Albert headed for Independence, Missouri, just outside of Kansas City.

Learning the Language and Baseball

CHAPTER THREE

Upon arriving in Independence, many of Albert's aunts and uncles found jobs as school bus drivers. For Albert, the toughest adjustments were not knowing anyone in Independence other than his family members and not being able to speak English.

He enrolled at Fort Osage High School, where he was classified as a sophomore—even though he was a year older than his classmates—because of his deficiency in language. He was assigned a tutor whom he worked with every day. He knew that being able to speak English would help out immensely in his goal to become a professional baseball player.

One of the first extracurricular activities that Albert inquired about upon enrolling at Fort Osage was its baseball team. His cousin, Wilfredo, introduced him

Did you know...?

Albert was a shortstop in high school and led his team, Fort Osage High School, to the Missouri state championship as a sophomore. As a junior, he walked 55 times in 88 plate appearances. He graduated at the end of the first semester of his senior year so he did not play as a senior.

to the coach, Dave Fry, who recalled the meeting well.

"He was tall and good looking, with big shoulders and a little waist," Fry said years later. "I told him, 'If you want to play, we're going to have a tryout session in February.' I didn't think about him anymore."

That was until February, when Fry became one of the first to realize that when Albert hits a baseball, a unique sound occurs when the ball meets the bat. Albert was in the gym, hitting, when Fry first heard that sound.

"I heard this 'whack, whack, whack,'" Fry said. "I thought, 'What in the world?' I went and took a look and Albert was in the cage, lining some shots. 'Gee, boy, what have we got here?' I said. He was a man among boys."

The hardest challenge for Fry was being able to communicate with Albert because of the language barrier.

"Any teaching, any communication, most of the time I would act it out or show him what I was trying to get across," Fry said. "He would keep me up all night taking ground balls, but his forte was hitting."

As hard as he worked on playing baseball, he worked just as hard at learning English. He was frustrated and exhausted at first, said his instructor, Portia Stanke, who taught English at the school, but he was determined to succeed because he knew how important it would be to his future success.

Stanke worked with him for the two and a half years he was a student at Fort Osage. Even though she knew how much he loved baseball, she was impressed with Albert's demeanor.

"Albert was always so proud to wear his baseball uniform to class the day he had a game," Stanke said. "But when he came back the next day, he never bragged about what he [had accomplished in a game]. You only knew if you asked him."

Fry told *Sports Illustrated*, "Language was Albert's biggest barrier. He had trouble understanding when you explained rules and regulations to him. But he loved baseball. You could get anything about baseball through to him, how to move his hands when he hit, where to set his feet when he was fielding."

Fry said there was little he tried to teach Albert about the game, except for one suggestion he made about where to put his hands when he was taking his stance.

"He held the bat up high and I said to him, 'You might find it helpful to lower your hands a bit.' That was it. Everything was natural for him."

It was his hitting ability that impressed Fry from the moment he saw him, and that impression has remained many years after Albert's short two-year stint on his team was completed.

"You only had to see Albert swing the bat once or twice to notice that he had some pretty good power," Fry said. "I never saw a kid swing so hard on every pitch. Not just once in a while, but every pitch. At our school, we have a short left field porch, and he constantly bombarded that house behind our fence."

Albert played shortstop in high school, but his real position was hitter. In his first season, he hit .471 with 11 home runs and 32 RBI as he led Fort Osage to the Missouri Class 4A state championship in 1997.

By the next season, 1998, when he was a junior, opposing coaches knew all about his offensive ability. He walked 55 times in only 88 plate appearances, showing even then that he was a disciplined hitter no matter how much he was frustrated. He still slammed eight homers in those 33 at-bats, including one Fry still remembers, on the road at Liberty High School.

The ball landed atop a 25-foot tall air conditioning unit that was on top of a building, about 40 feet beyond the left field fence. Observers estimated the blast had to travel at least 450 feet.

Albert the Great: The Albert Pujols Story

"The ball just traveled and traveled and traveled," Fry said. "I didn't think it would ever come down."

That was the exception that season, however, as more often than not Albert did not see any pitches that he could hit.

"They would let him bat one time and then walk him," Fry said. "Albert got pretty fed up with that. But if I was the opponent, I would have done it, too."

Despite his offensive display both seasons, Albert failed to make the Kansas City Star all-Metro team either year. As a junior, he was selected as the second-team shortstop, behind a player named Ryan Stegall of Liberty.

The main reason for that omission was that Albert had made more than 20 errors at shortstop, most of them throwing errors.

"Dominican players never actually set their feet," Fry said. "They're constantly throwing sidearm or underhanded. We were trying to get Albert to field the ball, go from the ground to the gut, point the shoulders and step and throw. That's a lot of things to say."

Scouts who began noticing Albert realized he was playing out of position at shortstop, but they also had a difficult time projecting a true and natural position for him. Also since he was only classified a junior because of the language issues, he was not eligible for the draft even though he was 18 years old.

The first time Mike Roberts, a cross-checker scout for the Cardinals, saw Albert was in the Area Code games the summer between his junior and senior year in high school. Roberts's brother-in-law, Dave Karaff, was the area scout for the Cardinals and had told him about the young slugger.

"The first thing you noticed about him was his strength," Roberts said. "He was not as big physically as he is now, but you could tell that he could hit."

However, Roberts and other scouts did not consider him a can't-miss-type prospect, mainly because of the questions about where he would play in the field.

"I know one guy who saw him and the only thing he wrote down on his report was 4.7, the time he ran going to first base," Roberts said. "He was not the kind of player that was going to blow you away when you first saw him. I just saw size and strength."

Aware of his desire to play professional baseball, some scouts advised Albert that he would have a better chance of being selected in the draft if he was able to graduate from high school early and enter a junior college. If he stayed in high school, he was told, teams would continue to pitch around him just as they had during his junior year. That would keep pro scouts from being able to get an accurate reading on his ability.

Those arguments were persuasive, and Albert gave up his senior season of baseball at Fort Osage to graduate at the end of the first semester.

In the fall of 1998, Albert played in an All-Star game for high schoolers in the Kansas City area and captured the attention of Marty Kilgore,

Did you know...?

Albert's first game for Maple Woods Community College was a smashing success. Playing shortstop, he turned an unassisted triple play and also hit a grand slam.

the coach at nearby Maple Woods Community College, a junior college.

"He was like a man playing with boys," Kilgore remembered, making the same statement Fry and other high school coaches had used.

Kilgore convinced Albert to attend Maple Woods, and he enrolled in January 1999 after graduating from high school. He again made an immediate impression.

One of Albert's new teammates was Landon Brandes, a sophomore and the team's leading hitter. Brandes would go on to join Albert in the Cardinals' minor league system as well.

"Everyone was using metal bats," Brandes said of the first practice when Albert joined the team. "Albert stepped in with a wood bat. I was hitting some out of the park before that, and I felt pretty good."

Albert proceeded to hit a ball that went at least 50 feet farther than any of the balls Brandes had hit. "Are you kidding me?" Brandes said to himself. "This kid is right out of high school and he's out-blasting me?"

For Kilgore, the difference once again was the sound. The way Albert hit the ball just sounded different. It was the same realization that Fry had had at Fort Osage, and the same realization the pros were going to come to in coming years.

"You don't hear that kind of explosion often," Kilgore said. In his first junior college game, Albert, still playing shortstop, turned an unassisted triple play and hit a grand slam. That was the start of a monster season, a .461 average with 22 homers and 80 RBIs.

The blast that people still talk about, like the high school home run hit at Liberty, came at Highland, Kansas, Community College. The ball sailed out of the park, across the street and into a tree. He also hit balls into people's yards and over houses.

Albert crushed one ball into a 30 mile-per-hour wind and got only a triple out of it. "He was pretty mad about it," Kilgore said. "He didn't think the wind should have mattered."

"He had baseball instincts that just couldn't be taught," Kilgore said. "The way he would run the bases, going from second to third when a third baseman came up throwing across ... just knowing how much to get off so they wouldn't throw behind him ... just the little things you can't teach that made him a special player. He was the best athlete I've ever seen with the baseball skills and power."

Albert led the Centaurs to a regional NJCAA championship, falling one game shy of making a trip to the national World Series. His ability became known among Maple Woods' opponents, and in one game against Seminole, Oklahoma, the team tried to keep Albert and Brandes from beating them by hitting them with a pitch every time they came up to bat.

"Every time they hit Albert, he would just stand there, look at them and stare them down," Kilgore said. "Nothing scares him."

Karaff, who began scouting for the Cardinals in 1996 after working for seven years with the Seattle Mariners, had seen Albert in high school and American Legion ball, but became more interested in him during his junior college season.

"He stood out more for me," Karaff said. "He hit some long home runs. You could see the power and the strength."

Karaff knew the Cardinals were not the only team watching Albert. The area scout for the Tampa Bay Devil Rays, in fact, had Albert listed as his number-one prospect and convinced the team to fly him to Tampa for a private workout prior to the June draft. The workout did not go well, however.

"For whatever reason the people in charge didn't care much for him,"

Karaff said. "He could just have had a bad day."

As Karaff knows, much of amateur scouting success is good luck, simply being in the right place at the right time when a player shows the ability to succeed at the professional level.

"I had never seen Albert strike out on a fastball, and the day I brought the regional crosschecker in to see him, he struck out twice on fastballs and in another at-bat fell down running over first base," Karaff said. "Luckily for me the scout came back the next day, too, and saw him hit one out of sight."

Karaff and Roberts both believed Albert had enough skills that he was worth selecting in the draft. Both expected him to go somewhere between the sixth and 10th rounds. After the 10th round was completed and Albert had not been chosen, Roberts—sitting in the Cardinals' draft room—began to lobby his bosses to select the young slugger.

Roberts still believes the reasons for the low selection was that Albert had again played shortstop in his only year in junior college, and scouts knew he would not be a shortstop in the pro ranks. He also had such limited exposure that scouts had not been able to give him a full evaluation.

"He moved okay, and he had a good enough arm that I thought he could maybe play third base," Roberts said. "I knew for sure he ought to be able to play first. What I saw I liked, but I knew what was going to carry him was his bat. I thought if he hit we could find a position for him to play.

"He was actually a better hitter with a wood bat then he was with an aluminum bat. He stayed back on the ball better. In the games he would drive some balls but he also struck out some."

Said Karaff, "I had some reservations about how well he was going to hit. I knew he would hit some home runs, and I didn't think he would strike out a lot, so I thought he was a guy worth taking a chance on."

Finally, in the 13th round, the Cardinals listened to Roberts and made the selection.

"We were lucky," Roberts said. "I think we got him because I happened to be there and had a chance to talk about him in the room. The area scout who had sent in all of the reports wasn't there, but because we had somebody who liked him there at the end, we were able to take him."

Albert was not disappointed he was chosen by the Cardinals, but was upset that all of the teams in baseball had passed over him for 12 rounds—choosing close to 400 other players—before his name was called. He was so upset he actually talked about giving up the sport he loved.

"It did bother me, I won't lie, I was disappointed," Albert said years later. "I thought maybe I should quit baseball."

He rejected the Cardinals' initial contract offer and moved west, agreeing to play for the collegiate summer league team in Hays, Kansas. There, he moved in with Frank and Barb Leo. Leo was the coach of the team.

Albert enjoyed a solid season, but impressed Leo more with his knowledge of the game and his maturity off the field.

"He was so aware of everything," Leo said, "how to hit certain kinds of pitchers, how to run the bases, how to play every situation. He came to us with a purpose in mind. He had a goal, and he wasn't going to be distracted from it."

It was a pep talk from his future mother-in-law that allowed Albert to forget about his disappointment over the draft results and sign with the Cardinals at the end of the 1999 summer season.

"I said, 'Albert, go, you love to play, you will prove yourself after you get there,'" said Linda Corona.

Albert listened to that advice.

"I prayed about it," he said. "God blessed me and gave me the chance. I decided I didn't care too much about where I got drafted. I knew if I was good enough, I would make it to the big leagues in three or four years."

Karaff signed him to a $65,000 package that included a signing bonus and money to pay for college expenses.

"He was such a great kid, I really liked him," Karaff said. "I knew he wanted to play, and we finally got it done."

Albert's childhood dream of one day becoming a professional baseball player was coming true.

"He had baseball instincts that

just couldn't be taught. He was

(M a r t y   K i l g o r e)

the best athlete I've ever seen."

A Minor Leaguer

CHAPTER FOUR

Albert did not join an established minor league team in 1999 because he signed so late in the season. Instead, he reported to the Cardinals' Instructional League team in Jupiter, Florida, where they annually bring in their top prospects.

He quickly made his presence known.

With minor league hitting instructor Mitchell Page observing, Albert used his first swing at Roger Dean Stadium to blast a line drive over the left field wall that smacked against the offices of the Montreal Expos, well beyond the outfield fence. He hit two other shots to the wall later in the day.

Mike Jorgensen, the Cardinals' director of player development, was sitting in the stands watching.

"In spring training you see the big boys popping the ball up there, but usually during the Instructional League you hardly see anybody who can hit it over the fence," Jorgensen said.

That night, Karaff received a phone call at his home from one of the Cardinals' minor league officials.

"Your boy had a pretty good day today," Karaff was told.

As Jorgensen continued to watch Albert for the next few days, he had a question for his scouts: "How come he wasn't drafted until the 13th round?" Jorgensen asked. "I was told some scouts thought he was heavy and didn't move that well, but everybody had to see the bat. It stood out that much. A lot of [other teams] missed the boat, but [we] were lucky to get him."

Albert continued to make a positive impression through the rest of the Instructional League, where he also received his first lessons in playing third base. He reported to the minor league camp for spring training in 2000 not knowing at what level the club wanted him to play that season.

It turned out to be Peoria, Illinois in the Class A Midwest League, a low-level Class A league. Many of the players at that level move up from the Rookie League programs but aren't considered polished enough to play at the high Class A level.

The team's manager was Tom Lawless, a former major league infielder with the Cardinals, who knew immediately that Albert was a superior talent to most of the players on his team and throughout the league.

"We knew he needed work on defense, but you could tell he was an outstanding hitter," Lawless said. "His mechanics were so good that he was taking the pitch from the

middle of the plate out and hitting it to right center and right field. That is usually a skill you have to teach young hitters; they normally try to pull everything.

"As the pitchers began to scout him, they started to work him inside more, and he was still trying to hit the pitch the other way. We had to teach him to get the barrel of the bat through the zone quicker so he could pull that pitch to left field. It didn't take him long to figure it out."

Albert began to make a name for himself by tearing through the Midwest League. He was named to the league's All-Star team and teamed with Hall of Famer Tony Perez to win the pregame home run-hitting contest.

Page, the roving instructor, came to Peoria and listed the hitters' names with a time he wanted to work with them. He omitted Albert's name because he was doing so well. Albert insisted he needed help and wanted the extra work with Page.

"He wasn't happy hitting .330 or .340 in A ball, so I gave him all the work he wanted," Page said.

The extra work definitely paid dividends.

"Once he figured it out, there was no question he would hit in the big leagues," Lawless said. "I thought he probably could have hit in the big leagues then, but he needed somewhere to play."

Lawless put in a lot of time working with Albert on playing third base. He had a plus arm to go with his above-average bat, but Lawless worried that the position would be too fast for him as he advanced through the system. That was his only concern.

"He was a very good student," Lawless said. "He worked hard and wanted to learn. He had the same problems a lot of young players have when he got frustrated and he didn't run out some ground balls. We had a little chat and took care of that. I told him, 'Don't make yourself look bad.' He was a good kid.

"It was his first year in pro baseball and he didn't really know what to expect, but he was very professional [in] the way he went about his business."

Albert was also earning money for the first time in his life, even though he and his new wife, Deidre, and their daughter lived in a sparsely furnished apartment, trying to get by on his check of $252 every two weeks.

He still was dreaming about the major leagues. Peoria was only a few hours north of St. Louis, so Albert was able to travel to St. Louis and sit in the stands at Busch Stadium for several Cardinals games when Peoria had a day off, thinking about the day when he would be down on the field playing.

The word about Albert's performance was making its way to the manager's office at Busch Stadium, too. One of his teammates at Peoria was Chris Duncan, the son of Dave Duncan, the Cardinals' pitching coach. It seemed that every time father and son talked, Chris was telling his dad about Albert's latest hitting feat.

Jorgensen was a frequent visitor to the games in Peoria not only because of Albert's presence, but because the Chiefs had anoth-

"It was his first year in pro baseball and he didn't really know what to expect, but he was very professional [in] the way he went about his business."

(T O M L A W L E S S)

A.J. WOLFE/THE COMMERCIAL APPEAL

er young outfield prospect, Ben Johnson, whom the Cardinals had drafted in the fourth round.

"San Diego had an area scout who lived around Peoria, and every time I was there, he was there, and that was not normally the case with area scouts," Jorgensen said. "It turned out we ended up talking with the Padres about a trade to bring in catcher Carlos Hernandez, and they wanted either Pujols or Johnson.

ABOVE: Albert became more renowned in the Cardinals' farm system after hitting a home run to capture the Pacific Coast League championship for Memphis in 2000.

"Pujols was still a little bit of a secret even though people knew about his numbers. Johnson's numbers were not quite as good, but we liked him a lot, too. We didn't want to trade either one of them, but we needed a backup catcher and we traded Johnson. Johnson reminds me a lot of Brian Jordan. He is still in San Diego's farm system, and I think has a chance to be a good player."

A few days before Albert was promoted from Peoria to the Cardinals' high Class A team in Potomac, Virginia, he left a memory for those in Peoria by blasting a home run high over the left field fence, landing on top of the team's dressing room, well behind the outfield wall.

"As well as he could hit going the opposite way, as soon as he learned to hit the inside pitch to left field, I knew he was on his way," Lawless said. "He has such strong hands, and his hand-eye coordination is so good, that was the secret to his success."

Before leaving in early August, Albert made enough of an impression around the league to be named the Most Valuable Player and share the honor of the league's top major league prospect with Reds outfielder Austin Kearns.

He left Peoria with a .324 average, 17 home runs and 84 RBIs in 109 games. He struck out only 37 times in 395 at-bats.

Arriving in Potomac, Albert continued doing exactly what he had been doing in Peoria. In the crowd for his first game happened to be Walt Jocketty, the Cardinals' general manager.

"He came to bat with runners in scoring position," Jocketty recalled. "I think he was behind in the count 1-2, and [he hit the] next pitch [for a] base hit up the middle for an RBI. Same thing with his next at-bat, in an almost identical situation. I said, 'Man this guy just gets off a plane, and he already is an RBI machine.'"

In 21 games before the end of the season, Albert hit a respectable .284 with two homers and 10 RBIs and again displayed good discipline by striking out only eight times in 81 at-bats.

Albert made an immediate impression on future Cardinals second baseman Bo Hart, who was playing at Potomac at that time.

"He hit the ball harder and more often than anyone I had ever seen," Hart said. "Anytime he made an out, it just seemed like someone accidentally was there to catch the ball."

When outfielder Ernie Young left the Triple A Memphis club to join the U.S. Olympic team, Memphis manager Gaylen Pitts put in a request to Jorgensen to add a righthanded hitter he could use off the bench for the Pacific Coast League playoffs.

"We knew for about three weeks Memphis was going to be playing Albuquerque and they had three lefthanded starters," Jorgensen said. "I was looking at the list of free agents and guys who had been released, and Pitts finally said to me one day, 'What about Pujols?'"

Jorgensen told him that Albert had only one year of experience, all at the Class A level, but Pitts suggested that Albert be promoted to Memphis to give him a few days to acclimate himself to Triple A. Then they could make a decision about whether he could play at that level before the playoff roster had to be set. Jorgensen agreed, and Albert was on his way to Memphis.

"The thing you worry about with a young player is moving him [up] too quickly, before he is ready. But you could tell Pujols was a special hitter," Jorgensen said. "And he had had such a great season, I think it would have been hard to break his confidence."

Albert played well enough to be added to the playoff roster, even though he was playing left field after playing third base all season. Pujols quickly showed he was able to compete at that advanced level, hitting .302 in 11 postseason games. He capped off his performance by slamming a game- and pennant-winning homer in the 13th inning to give Memphis a 4-3 win over Salt Lake City and the Pacific Coast League championship. Albert was named the MVP of the playoffs.

"He was kind of a one-man wrecking crew," Jorgensen said. "By then you could tell he was going to be a special player and not just a special hitter. I really have to give a lot of credit to Pitts for wanting him and giving him a chance at that level."

Albert's year wasn't over, however, as he moved farther west to Scottsdale, Arizona, to play in the Arizona Fall League as one of the game's best prospects. He hit .323 with four homers and 21 RBIs in 27 games and was voted by the league's managers and coaches as the best third base prospect in the league. He was one of only three players named on every ballot.

Albert's baseball future looked very bright, but he had not saved enough money to get him and his young family through the winter, so the family moved in with his wife's parents in Kansas City and he got a job at Meadowbrook Country Club. His job was to set up rooms for parties and other catering functions.

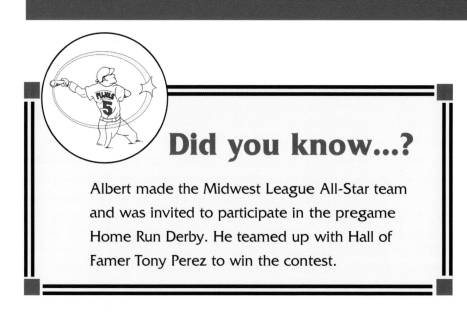

Did you know...?

Albert made the Midwest League All-Star team and was invited to participate in the pregame Home Run Derby. He teamed up with Hall of Famer Tony Perez to win the contest.

When he wasn't working at his job, however, Albert was working on his baseball skills. The Cardinals were projecting that he would bypass the Double A level and open the 2001 season back at Triple A Memphis, just one short step away from the major leagues.

As he reported to his first big league spring training camp, Albert was aware of the Cardinals' game plan, but he also knew that sometimes plans could be changed.

ABOVE: Albert made the rare jump from Class A to Triple A Memphis, where he hit .302 in 11 postseason games.

Albert the Great: The Albert Pujols Story

Making the Cut

CHAPTER FIVE

Heading into spring training in the year 2001, Cardinals executives who had read all of the minor-league reports on Albert—but had yet to see him in action—were anxious to get their first live look. Everyone knew the plan was to send him back to the minors, but that didn't change their desire to see how he matched up against major league talent.

Albert was assigned uniform number 68—a high number—which was a pretty good indication that he did not figure in the team's immediate major league plans. The Cardinals' regular third baseman the previous year, Fernando Tatis, had been traded to Montreal over the winter, leaving veterans Craig Paquette and Placido Polanco as the favorites to share time at the hot corner. The Cardinals remained firm in their belief that Albert could be the third baseman of the future, but the future was likely at least a year away.

SCOTT ROVAK

Albert, however, reported to Jupiter, Florida, with other ideas in mind. His goal was to play well enough to force manager Tony La Russa and the Cardinals to keep him on the major league roster.

When the pitchers began throwing live batting practice in late February, Albert received his first opportunity to make an impression. Pitching coach Dave Duncan was closely watching his pitchers; but his eyes also wandered to Albert.

"He was taking really professional at-bats," Duncan said. "You could tell he was determined to compete, even in those situations. He wasn't going to do something in the cage in February that was going to create a bad habit or give a bad impression."

La Russa began to notice him as well, not only in the batting cage but during the other early spring drills.

"You watched him do the things and said, 'Man, there's some talent here. This guy's got a chance,'" La Russa said. "Wonder how long it will be before he gets to the big leagues?"

Injuries to Mark McGwire and Bobby Bonilla gave La Russa an excuse and an opportunity to put Albert into spring training games. He took full advantage of the opening.

Albert was rooming with his college and minor league teammate, Landon Brandes, who was in the club's minor league camp. Each night back at the hotel they would discuss their performances that day.

"He'd say, 'Tomorrow I'm going to go out and get a couple of hits,'" Brandes said. "He knew what kind of game plan he would

have already. It wasn't him being cocky. It was just him saying, 'This is my job, to get a couple of hits and a couple of RBIs.'"

La Russa began playing Albert in the outfield and at first base in addition to his work at third base. Early in the spring, he made a diving catch in the outfield with the bases loaded to take a hit away from the Mets' Mike Piazza. La Russa's coaches insisted that the manager was looking for an excuse to send Albert back to the minors by playing him so often and in different positions, waiting for him to fail. La Russa acknowledged he was giving the youngster a stern test.

"It was impossible to get him to perform poorly, and I pushed him," La Russa said.

"Dave Duncan accused me of trying to find a place where he couldn't play, but Albert refused to cooperate. I kept using him against the toughest pitchers, and he kept hitting."

General manager Walt Jocketty said as the club began to cut its roster by sending players to the minors, each week Albert's name came up and the reaction was always the same: "Nope, we can't cut him this week."

The Cardinals at the time shared their spring training complex with the Montreal Expos, and played them more than any other opponent. Another manager who kept watching Albert was the Expos' Felipe Alou.

"I saw a lot of Albert," Alou said. "Tony (La Russa) and I are pretty close, and one day he asked me, 'Do you like that kid?'"

RIGHT: The uniform—number 68—reveals that the Cardinals did not expect Albert to make the club in spring training of 2001.

SCOTT ROVAK

"He was talking about Pujols, and I told him that I liked him a lot. It seemed like everything he hit that spring was hard. As spring training came to a close, Tony told me he was thinking about carrying the kid on the roster, even though he lacked experience. ... He's truly what I would call a phenom with a bat. One year out of Class A, and he was hitting like that."

After Albert had been playing a great deal, La Russa gave him a day off on a trip to Viera, about two hours away, to play the Florida Marlins. Albert was on the trip, but La Russa said he should not expect to play in the game but might be called on to pinch-hit late in the game.

"He said, 'Okay,'" La Russa said. "We had the field for an hour (before the game) and he took groundballs at shortstop for an hour. I said, 'Albert, this is your day off.' He said, 'No, I played short in college.' He was catching and throwing. The guy just likes to play baseball."

The next day La Russa put Albert at shortstop and he started a double play on the first ball hit to him.

La Russa still intended to send Albert to Memphis for the regular season until about 10 days remained in spring training. The Cardinals traveled to Lake Buena Vista to play the Atlanta Braves at the Disney Sports Complex. It was a Sunday game, and La Russa played most of his projected regulars. Albert did not start.

Sitting on the bench late in the game, McGwire began asking La Russa about Albert and whether he was going to make the club. The manager told McGwire that he really needed a spot to play him; even if he was one of the top 25 players in camp, he preferred that he play every day in Triple A instead of riding the bench in the majors.

In the ninth inning, La Russa sent Albert up to pinch-hit against a righthanded pitcher who had major league experience. He drove a high fastball over the scoreboard in center field. McGwire was sitting next to La Russa in the dugout. As the ball was clearing the scoreboard, McGwire was jamming his elbow into the manager's side. "Did you see that? How are you not going to take him?"

McGwire told his manager that if Albert did not make the club, La Russa would be making a big mistake.

Still, La Russa did not want to keep Albert unless he had a place for him to play. Finally, a spot opened up at the end of camp

RIGHT: Albert's willingness to learn new positions—which led to his versatility on defense—was one of the factors that aided him in making the big league club in 2001.

Did you know...?

Albert was assigned uniform number 68 for his first spring training with the Cardinals. He switched to uniform number 5 after making the team by hitting .349, leading the team with 34 total bases and striking out only eight times in 62 at-bats.

when Bonilla suffered a pulled hamstring and had to be placed on the disabled list.

Albert, after hitting .349, leading the club with 34 total bases and having struck out only eight times in 62 spring training at-bats, had made the major league roster with only three games of regular-season experience above the Class A level.

La Russa, however, tried to caution Albert that the move was only guaranteed through the opening series in Colorado and that another decision could be made if Bonilla became healthy enough to play in a few days.

Albert turned in his number 68 jersey and was issued a new jersey with the number 5 on the back. He had made the team, and he knew he was not going to give up his status as a major leaguer easily.

Rookie of the Year

The Cardinals opened the 2001 season on April 2 in Colorado, and Albert found himself in the opening-day lineup, playing left field and batting sixth. Just 361 days earlier, he had made his professional debut, playing in a game for the Peoria Chiefs.

Albert was about to prove that the higher level didn't make any difference to him. He was still just playing baseball, the same game he had been playing virtually all his life. The fact he was playing on a bigger stage was not an obstacle. He was confident in his ability, and those around him soon realized his work ethic was going to make up for whatever difference did exist in talent level.

Albert collected his first major league hit that day, a single off the Rockies' Mike Hampton, one of five hits the Cardinals recorded as Hampton pitched Colorado to an 8-0 victory. The Rockies went on to

sweep the three-game series, and Albert was held hitless in the next two games, carrying a one for nine performance with him as the Cardinals' road trip continued at Arizona.

No doubt many rookies would have been worried, especially when their status as a major leaguer was kind of tentative anyway, but not Albert.

"I was hitting the ball good, so I didn't get frustrated," Albert said. "I knew what I could do. I just let it happen and had a good series at Arizona."

The Arizona series, in fact, was what launched Albert onto the national stage as a player to watch. He went seven for 14 in the series, hit his first major leaguer homer, off Armando Reynoso, and drove in eight runs. His biggest hit, however, came against a future Hall of Famer, Randy Johnson, in the final game of the series.

The Cardinals pounded Johnson for nine runs that day, the most he had given up in 193 starts. Albert slammed a two-out, two-strike two-run double that earned him a photo in that week's story about the Cardinals in *Sports Illustrated.*

"After grounding out in my first at-bat of the season, I said to myself, 'Okay, just relax and play the game like you always do,'" Albert said. "That's what I'm doing."

Said McGwire, "When he bombed the double off the wall in center off Randy Johnson, we all went, 'Uh-oh. We've got something here.'"

The next day, Albert became the first Cardinals rookie to hit a home run in the team's home opener since Wally Moon in 1954. His first month in the major leagues included a 13-game hitting streak, and he tied the major-league rookie record for most home runs in April with eight, joining Kent Hrbek and Carlos Delgado in the record book.

As McGwire continued to struggle in his recovery from surgery, La Russa was left with little choice but to move Albert into the cleanup spot in the batting order, but it seemed to make no difference to Albert. He had the first two-homer game of his career en route to being named the NL Rookie of the Month. Facing Johnson for a second time, he extended a game-winning rally with a single to the opposite field after having struck out twice earlier in the game.

"Two strikes, ball away, that's what he does," La Russa said. "Hitting in the four spot, he's not fazed."

Albert finished April with a .370 average and in 24 games drove in 27 runs and scored 18 runs to go along with his eight homers. He led the team in RBIs, homers, runs and games played.

Albert's performance was not lost on his teammates.

"There's no awe in his eyes," said second baseman Fernando Vina.

Added utility player Larry Sutton, "He's the type of kid who will sit next to you and ask questions. He doesn't act presumptuous. He doesn't act like he's been in the big leagues for 10 years. He's in the cage 24 hours a day and wants to get better. That's all you can ask for from a young player."

Did you know...?

In 2001, Albert became the ninth player in National League history to be named the Rookie of the Year in a unanimous vote.

Naturally, there were some skeptics who were adopting a wait-and-see attitude about Albert's performance. One of them was Arizona manager Bob Brenly, who said after the team's second series against the Cardinals that he thought Albert was benefiting from nobody in the league having much of a scouting report on him.

"We just don't know the kid," Brenly said at the time. "The series we had in Arizona, we just had bad scouting reports. We ended up throwing the ball right where he likes it—a lot. That being said, we went back and watched the tape and he also hit some good pitches.

"He's obviously a physically gifted young man. A lot of rookies come up at this level and feel overmatched. They're not sure if they belong or can compete at this level. Other rookies come up with that little edge, that confidence, that look in their eye that they belong. He certainly has that look."

Injuries to McGwire, Jim Edmonds and J.D. Drew depleted the Cardinals' offensive attack, putting even more responsibility on Albert's shoulders as he became the cleanup hitter. He didn't seem to notice.

"Putting a rookie [in the cleanup spot] is not what you want to do," La Russa said. "I think that's what has been hard, that he's hit in the middle of the lineup and pitchers have been concentrating on him from the first month of the season. And he still has great at-bats. ... I've never seen anyone this mature with so little experience and for being so young."

Like Brenly, there were other skeptics around the league who believed Albert would struggle once teams were able to scout him and get more information about how to pitch to him. Had that happened, he would not have been the first rookie to get off to a hot start and then fizzle.

Once teams discovered more about Albert, however, they learned that he was not going to fizzle. One of the keys to his remarkable success as a rookie was his consistency.

He followed up his success in April by hitting .333 in May with eight homers and 24 RBIs. He then hit .330 in June with five homers and 15 RBIs, both highs for the team.

Even when Bobby Bonilla came back off the disabled list, there was no doubt Albert was not going anywhere. Instead the club designated John Mabry for assignment

and later sold his contract to the Florida Marlins.

"I'm glad things worked out the way they did, because he had just as good a spring as anybody on the team, if not the best spring," Bonilla said. "He's going to do a lot more in this game, because his upside is huge. The most impressive thing about him is how he's been able to keep things on an even keel."

One of the early believers was Cardinals hitting coach Mike Easler.

"People are going to be paying just to see Albert Pujols one day," Easler said. "That's how good he is. There's a confidence about him. It's not cockiness. He has a quiet confidence that tells you he expects to be here a long time."

Easler, a former major leaguer himself, was not shy in his praise for Albert and his comparison to former star hitters, including Hall of Famers. Like many of those who had been around Albert at different levels, Easler said it was the sound of the ball hitting his bat that made the biggest impression on him.

"Only a few guys can make that sound," Easler said. "Willie Stargell, Dave Parker, Dave Winfield, Mike Schmidt. I'm talking about guys like that. The ball just explodes off his bat, and he's talented enough that he can take his power swing and make adjustments and go the other way for a base hit.

RIGHT: It didn't take Albert's new teammates—including veteran pitcher Darryl Kile—long to warm to him thanks to his work ethic, steady performance and modest attitude.

Albert the Great: The Albert Pujols Story

"People are going to be paying just to see Albert Pujols one day. That's how good he is. ...He has a quiet confidence that tells you he

(MIKE EASLER)

expects to be here a long time."

"I can tell him something in between at-bats about how a pitcher is trying to work him and he can make the adjustments just that quick. The next at-bat, he'll do exactly what you've talked to him about. It's just amazing how polished he is at such a young age."

Proving that he was human, Albert did suffer the first prolonged slump of his career in early July as talk was building about his chances of making the National League All-Star team—even though he was not on the ballot. On a nine-game trip leading up to the All-Star break, Albert was just two for 33, including zero for 12 with runners in scoring position, and his season average dipped from .354 to .323.

That slump did not diminish his accomplishments in the first half of the season, however, and Albert was selected as a reserve for the All-Star game in Seattle by manager Bobby Valentine of the

Mets. He became the first Cardinals rookie since pitcher Luis Arroyo in 1955 to be selected for the game, and when he entered the game as a replacement for Jeff Kent, he became the first Cardinals rookie to actually play in an All-Star game since third baseman Eddie Kazak in 1949.

Albert drew a walk from the Mariners' Jeff Nelson in his only plate appearance.

The trip to the All-Star game and recognition as one of the game's elite players capped an unbelievable first half of the season for Albert. With half a season remaining, he had already tied the team's rookie record for home runs in a season with 21, matching the total set by Ray Jablonski in 1953. He hit the All-Star break leading all major league rookies in home runs, RBIs, on-base percentage and slugging percentage.

Remarkably, Albert was able to concentrate offensively despite being shuffled through various positions on defense. In the first half of the year he started 46 games at third base, 14 in right field, 13 at first base, six in left field and two as a designated hitter.

"I don't care where I play," Albert said. "I know sometimes I make mistakes, but that's going to happen. When I get older, I am going to get better."

That statement of confidence might have come off wrong if it had come from many other people, but with Albert, almost every observer accepted it merely as a statement of fact. And he went out the rest of the season continuing to prove his case. As manager Tony La Russa shuffled Albert from position to position throughout the remainder of the season, he continued to hit.

Did you know...?

Albert has recorded only one sacrifice bunt in his career, as a rookie in 2001.

The Cardinals had been a .500 team during the first half of the season and found themselves in third place, eight games out of first, at the All-Star break. They began to climb back into the pennant race in August, however, as they enjoyed a 20-10 month. Albert was enjoying another banner month, too. In August, he contributed a 17-game hitting streak and a 453-foot homer at Busch Stadium against the Marlins, the longest home run by a Cardinal in 2001. On August 29 he hit his 31st homer of the season and joined Jablonski as the only Cardinal rookie to ever drive in more than 100 runs in his debut season.

The Cardinals finished August with a 73-61 record, but still found themselves six games out of first. A nine-game winning streak in September thrust them into the middle of the NL Central and the wild card race, and earned Albert recommendations not only for Rookie of the Year, almost a foregone conclusion, but for serious MVP consideration.

"I really believe the stats don't come anywhere close to telling the story of how this guy's played," La Russa said. "That he's been able to maintain this for six months … I don't care if you've been in the league 10 years, he's had a phenomenal season.

"I've been fortunate and had some MVP performances. I think of (Carlton) Fisk (whom La Russa managed with the White Sox). Harold Baines. Jose Canseco. Mark McGwire. Rickey Henderson. But I don't know anybody who has had a better year

than this guy. He's been as good as any I've been fortunate to see. … What this kid has done is the greatest performance of any position player I've ever seen."

Albert's heralded teammate, McGwire, said Albert should pull the same double-award that Fred Lynn did for the Boston Red Sox in 1975, winning both the MVP and the Rookie of the Year awards in the American League.

"There's no doubt in my mind that if we make the playoffs, Albert Pujols should be an MVP candidate," McGwire said. "He respects everything but is in awe of almost nothing."

The Cardinals had won three consecutive games in early September, moving them into second place and five games out of first, when the season was interrupted for a week because of the September 11 terrorist attacks. They won the next six games when play resumed, including a game at Pittsburgh when Albert broke a 5-5 tie in the ninth with his first career grand slam.

When the Cardinals reeled off another six-game winning streak at the end of the month they found themselves tied with Houston for first with five games to play.

When the Astros won two of the final three games, the two teams finished with matching 93-69 records, although Houston was declared the division champion by virtue of winning the season series against the Cardinals. The Cardinals, however,

AP/WWP

qualified for postseason play for the second consecutive year by claiming the wild card.

Albert was once again featured in an article in *Sports Illustrated*, and by now his performance was not a secret. He had just completed what many longtime observers believed was the greatest rookie season in baseball history.

"I believe he's been reincarnated, that he played before, in the 1920s and 1930s,"

McGwire said. "He's back to prove something. He fits every definition of what the MVP should be. If we didn't have him, well, I don't want to think where we'd be."

McGwire knew about great rookie seasons, having set the record for most home runs by a rookie when he blasted 49 for Oakland in 1987. He did not have the other numbers, however, to equal Albert's overall performance.

"He doesn't take anything for granted.

He asks questions, and he's willing to

try and accept anything you throw at
(J I M   E D M O N D S)

him. That's why he's being successful."

The list of records was long and impressive, but Albert insisted that was not a motivating factor behind his success.

"I don't try to think about records," he said. "I don't think about what Ted Williams did or what Frank Robinson did. I'm not trying to have a great year as a rookie setting records. I am trying to get my baseball team into the playoffs and World Series. That is the only record that I want."

The team did make the playoffs, but fell short of Albert's goal of reaching the World Series when it lost a riveting five-game, first-round series to the Arizona Diamondbacks, who went on to win the world championship.

Albert struggled in those games, collecting only two hits (one a home run) in 18 at-bats. That disappointment, however, could not take away from or diminish his accomplishments in the regular season.

Did you know...?

Albert's 130 RBIs in 2001 tied him in Cardinals history with Enos Slaughter for the 12th highest RBI total in a season. Of the players ranked above him, all but Mark McGwire and Joe Torre are in the Hall of Fame.

RIGHT: During his rookie season, Albert quickly proved he was a well-rounded player and not just an exceptional hitter.

"He doesn't look at it as having success but feels he's just doing his job," said teammate Jim Edmonds. "He doesn't take anything for granted. He asks questions, and he's willing to try and accept anything you throw at him. That's why he's being successful."

The numbers were staggering. Albert became only the fifth rookie to lead the Cardinals in batting average for a season, the first since Bake McBride did it in 1974. He was the seventh rookie to lead the team in homers, the first since Todd Zeile in 1990. He was only the third rookie to lead the team in RBIs and the first since Joe Medwick in 1933. The only other rookie to lead the team in all three Triple Crown categories was Rogers Hornsby in 1916. He was the first Cardinal player to win the team's Triple Crown since Ted Simmons did it 1973.

SCOTT ROVAK

He became only the fourth rookie in history and the first in the National League to hit .300 with 30 homers, 100 RBIs and 100 runs scored, matching the accomplishment of Cleveland's Hal Trotsky in 1934, Boston's Ted Williams in 1939, and Boston's Walt Dropo in 1950. The last Cardinals player to accomplish that feat was Stan Musial in 1952. The last Cardinal to lead the team in those same four categories in the same year was Ken Boyer in 1961.

Albert set the Cardinals rookie records for home runs, doubles, RBIs, extra-base hits, runs and total bases. He established National League rookie records for RBIs, extra base hits and total bases.

Albert finished in the NL's top 10 in batting average, RBIs, multi-hit games, total bases, doubles, on-base percentage, slugging percentage, extra base hits, and game-winning RBIs.

He became the ninth unanimous selection as Rookie of the Year and finished fourth in the MVP award balloting.

It was his ability to ignore his personal statistics and success and focus on the team's success, however, that impressed and pleased his veteran teammates and manager.

"A lot of people have been pushing him," said catcher Mike Matheny. "If they see something that isn't quite right, they call him out. They're trying to help him out. At first, it's hard to have people keep getting on you. But he's taking some of the things these guys are telling him, as far as the coaches and some of the veterans go, and it's making him a better player."

Said La Russa, "The message we send to all our players, but particularly a guy like Albert having so much success, is that you've got to dedicate yourself to professionalism and excellence. And it sounds corny, but that's a tough message nowadays. That's not what players hear from their representatives."

Albert listened to both his teammates and his manager, because he knew his goals were not complete after only one season. There would be additional years, and he knew more challenges would come his way.

"Everything about Albert is legitimate," La Russa said. "He could do this for

RIGHT: Albert and his wife, Deidre, smile as they arrive at a news conference in St. Louis announcing Albert as the recipient of the National League Rookie of the Year award.

AP/WWP

a long time. The two biggest issues that could get in the way of him having a great career are first, that he's a big guy. We saw in spring training that he had a really good winter training and stayed in shape. He was quick. The older you get, the tougher it is to carry weight. So he will have to keep up that kind of work.

"Second, maybe most important, is the atmosphere today in the major leagues that if a guy is successful, even if he is just a little successful, much less incredibly successful, he will face a lot of pressure to focus on (outside influences)."

As Albert prepared for his second season, he was determined to prove he could withstand that pressure.

Building on Success

CHAPTER SEVEN

Albert was determined not to be a one-year wonder. He worked out incredibly hard in the offseason, preparing for the 2002 campaign.

He had already earned the respect and admiration not only of his teammates but of opponents. If anything, that status only increased when they realized that Albert was not resting on his laurels after his rookie success.

"You look at how far he has come as a player in two years," said catcher Mike Matheny, a frequent workout partner of Albert during the winter. "He's a central player on this team. There are people coming at him from every angle who want something from him. To his credit, he's been able to keep his focus. Some people may have trouble understanding that, but there's probably no way he can make everyone happy."

The person Albert was most determined to make happy was himself, and that would come by improving on his rookie season. That would seem like an almost impossible task, but it didn't seem that way to Albert, who thought there were many things he could learn that would make him a better and more productive hitter.

He constantly studies hitters on opposing teams, looking for tips and ideas that he can adapt to his own game.

"You look at the best hitters from Chicago, Houston, Arizona … and you try to learn something from them," he said. "I do that with every team we play. I've got a lot of respect watching (Todd) Helton every time we play Colorado.

"I learn something new every time I walk into a park. You learn from your mistakes and things that happen. Every day, you learn something new, and that's what you want to do to get better and better."

One star who gave some advice to Albert was Alex Rodriguez. He taught Albert a tee drill that he now uses to help him keep his swing under control.

Albert understood that as quickly as he had become a star, that fame could just as easily fade away—and he was not about to let that happen.

"I don't want to throw this opportunity away," he said. "I don't want to be lazy in this game. I don't want to be cocky. I don't want to think that I'm the best. I always want to be humble and be the same guy I was three or four years ago, when I signed, through the minor leagues and here in the big leagues."

And as he would continue to prove over the next few years, Albert's goals were almost always team-oriented. He was disappointed by his performance in the first-round playoff loss to Arizona the previous year, and one of his motivating goals was to help the Cardinals return to the playoffs in 2002 so he would have another chance for success.

What he and the rest of the Cardinals did not count on when the season began was that they would also have to overcome tragedy. First, longtime broadcaster Jack Buck passed away, and just days later pitcher Darryl Kile was found dead in his hotel room while the Cardinals were playing in Chicago.

The shocking and stunning death of Kile would have been a valid reason for the team to collapse during the second half of the season, but instead, Albert and his teammates used it as motivation, saying they were now playing "for Darryl."

When the regular season was over, Albert once again found himself ranked among the NL leaders in almost every offensive category, and the Cardinals were headed back to the playoffs as the Central Division champions.

After becoming the first Cardinal to lead the team in average, home runs, RBI and runs in 40 years as a rookie, Albert duplicated that feat. He became the first player in major league history to hit at least .300 with 30 homers, 100 RBIs and 100 runs scored in each of his first two seasons. He was one of only four players in the league to finish in the top 10 in the three

Triple Crown categories, joining MVP Barry Bonds, Vladimir Guerrero and Jeff Kent.

Albert became the first hitter since Ted Williams in 1939-40 to drive in more than 250 runs in his first two seasons in the majors. Only two other players—Joe DiMaggio and Dale Alexander—had performed that feat prior to Williams.

Albert improved from fourth to second in the MVP voting, and became the first Cardinal since Musial in 1950-51 to finish in the top four in the balloting in consecutive years.

One newcomer who received a first-hand appreciation of Albert was Scott Rolen, acquired by the Cardinals from the Phillies in July. Rolen had played against Albert for a year and a half, but gained extra respect watching him on a daily basis.

"You see him twice a year and you figure you're catching him when he's hot," Rolen said. "When you're on the same team, you realize he's like that every day. You think he has to cool off sometimes, but he doesn't. He's that good.

"He has a knack of controlling the at-bat instead of the pitcher controlling the at-bat. The pitcher needs to make adjustments. The other thing is, he has the ability of knowing where that bat head is and getting that bat head to the ball. Barry (Bonds) hits so many balls on the barrel. That's the way Albert is. You can throw him an inside pitch, and he might hit a home run to right field. He's not concerned about pulling the ball."

What Albert was concerned about was not having another disappointing post-season. The Cardinals again played the

Did you know...?

In 2002, Albert finished second in MVP voting to Barry Bonds. Albert is the fourth Cardinal to finish in the top five in MVP voting for four consecutive years, and the first to do so since Stan Musial, who did it for five consecutive years between 1948 and 1952.

"You see him twice a year and you figure you're catching him when he's hot. When you're on the same team, you realize he's like that every day. You think he has to cool off sometimes,

(S C O T T   R O L E N)

but he doesn't. He's that good."

LEFT: Albert reacts after another big hit in the clutch—a game-winning single against the Pirates on July 27, 2003.

Diamondbacks in the first round of the playoffs, and Albert had three hits, including a triple, as the Cardinals swept Arizona in three games to advance to the National League Championship Series. Unfortunately, they lost Rolen due to an injury, and that hurt them against the Giants. San Francisco beat the Cardinals in five games to win the pennant and advance to the World Series, denying the Cardinals what they thought would have been a fitting tribute to Kile and Buck by winning the world championship.

As he looked back on his first two seasons, however, Albert could find satisfaction in the knowledge that almost no one in baseball history had had more individual success in his first two seasons. On top of that, the Cardinals had made three consecutive playoff appearances for the first time since 1942-44.

But he knew that he and the team could do better, and he set out to prove that in 2003.

To do that, he knew he would have to continue to make adjustments in his style of hitting, because pitchers were constantly changing their approach to him, trying to find a weakness to exploit and new ways to try to get him out.

"The pitchers in this league have tried to throw him up and in, low and away, sinkers and sliders," said hitting coach Mitchell Page. "They've thrown the kitchen sink at him, and they've never been able to solve him. He's adjusted to everything."

Said Mets pitcher Tom Glavine: "What makes him special is that things come naturally. It's no big overhaul in his swing to hit the ball with power the other way. You can't just work him away and hope for a single, you're just as fearful that he'll hit a home run to the opposite field."

Albert learned in his first two seasons that continuing to be able to adjust to the pitchers' strategies was going to be necessary if he was going to be the player he wanted to be.

"That's how you become a good hitter," he said, "when you can tell yourself what you're doing wrong and correct it the next at-bat. You don't want to do the same thing in three at-bats … then do something different the last at-bat. By then, it's too late.

"You want to make adjustments your first at-bat. You don't have to wait until somebody else corrects it. Sometimes it's better for people outside to say something, but 90 percent of the time I know what I'm

RIGHT: Albert tries to give back to the fans by signing as many autographs as he can before games.

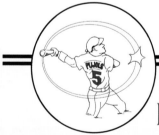

Did you know...?

Albert owns the fourth-best season in Cardinals history in terms of total bases, with 394 in 2003. Rogers Hornsby set the team record of 450 in 1922. Stan Musial with 429 (in 1948) and Joe Medwick with 406 (in 1937) rank second and third ahead of Albert.

Albert the Great: The Albert Pujols Story

AP/WWP

doing wrong. I don't do much with my arms and legs. I'm quiet."

Only a perfectionist could find that Albert was doing anything wrong at all. He began to pick up more national attention and acclaim when he starred at the Home Run Derby the day before the 2003 All-Star game in Chicago. He hit a record-tying 14 homers in the semifinal round, but lost 9-8 to Anaheim's Garret Anderson in the finals.

The All-Star appearance capped a brilliant first half of the season when he hit .368 with 27 homers and 86 RBIs, numbers many players would have been happy with for the entire season. He led all National League players in fan balloting for the game, collecting more than two million votes.

He continued to earn praise and respect from older and more experienced players, who sought him out for hitting tips

and advice. One player who said his offensive performance improved after talking to Albert was Reds first baseman Sean Casey, who sought out Albert for advice even though he is six years older than Albert and hit .332 in 1999 while Albert was playing in junior college.

"You talk to him about hitting, and you can't believe you're listening to a 23-year-old guy," Casey said. "He has such a good idea about it all—staying inside the ball, hitting in counts, covering the plate with two strikes, his approach.

"It's amazing how much he already knows, how much he's figured out."

What Albert really had figured out was that he was blessed by God to be able to play baseball, and that his hard work and concentration were the continuing keys for his success.

"God gave me this natural ability," Albert said. "But it's even better when you work hard and you put those two things together. (Then) it's unbelievable ... I've been blessed. I don't know how. The main thing is I can read a pitcher. I can make adjustments. People wonder how I am able to do that. I don't know. I can't explain. ... I try to see the ball and have a plan."

Pitchers always have a plan when they are facing any hitter, but what most of the pitchers around the N.L. learned after battling Albert was that their plan oftentimes didn't work.

"He is a tough guy to feel like you've got a game plan to get out," said Glavine. "He's one of those rare guys who hits for power and average and doesn't strike out."

Added Cubs pitcher Kerry Wood, "I'm most impressed by his ability not to swing at balls out of the strike zone. It's amazing to have such discipline at that age. With his ability, you take your chances and try to get him to chase a pitch. But usually he doesn't."

Even though Albert's teammates continued to be impressed, they began to accept his performance as normal and not extraordinary.

"It's gotten to the point where you don't even marvel at it anymore," said first baseman Tino Martinez. "You just kind of expect it. Yeah, you expect him to hit home runs. You expect him to drive in runs, and you expect him to have great at-bats every time. We're just used to seeing it.

"I've played with great, great players, guys who put up some good numbers. But I've never seen a guy as focused as he is. The focus is unbelievable."

In addition to his remarkable focus and concentration, the other component of Albert's game that most observers thought was a key to his success was his quick hands and strong arms. He has the ability to take an inside pitch and still get his hands through the hitting zone quick enough that the barrel of the bat connects squarely with the ball, allowing it to stay fair and not be yanked foul.

"It's amazing to see what he does on balls that are inside, in off the plate, than balls that are outside and away from him," said Cubs pitcher Mark Prior. "He just drives everything. It's amazing to see how well he gets his hands inside the ball."

When Albert and the Cardinals played the Baltimore Orioles in an interleague game, then-manager Mike Hargrove came away from watching Albert very impressed.

"Our closer, Jorge Julio, was throwing 97-98 [miles per hour] and started him off with a nasty first-pitch slider," Hargrove said. "Pujols missed it by three feet. He came back with a 97-mph fastball just above the belt, in, and he turned on it and hit a triple down the left field line. I don't know many people who can do that. He goes from being made to look like a fool on a slider to coming back and hitting the 97-mph heater that's inside, off the plate a little bit. That's just getting your hands to the ball a lot better than anybody else."

Albert knows how important his hands are. Even though he is reluctant to talk about himself or his hitting "secrets," he did admit that he thinks his performance is directly related to his hands.

"The key to hitting is hands," he said. "You leave your hands back so even if you jump at the ball, your hands are back. If it's a breaking ball, you can still put a good swing on it. Sometimes you're going to get fooled on a breaking ball. Then you adjust the next pitch. But what's most important is for my hands to be in the right position for me to drive the ball.

"If it's away, I can drive the ball away. If it's inside, I can pull the ball down the line."

Hall of Famer Red Schoendienst, still active with the Cardinals, was a teammate of three of the greatest hitters in the history of baseball—Musial with the Cardinals, Hank Aaron with the Braves and Willie Mays with the Giants. He sees a favorable comparison between Albert and those all-time greats.

"I look at Albert from the elbows down and it's obvious he has tremendous strength," Schoendienst said. "That's where you generate power... just look at all the great hitters, they had tremendous power in their forearms, hands and wrists. Albert is like that."

People did not know how Albert could improve given his success during his first two years in the majors, but he showed how in 2003.

His 2003 season was one of the best individual years in Cardinals history as he hit .359 with 43 homers, 124 RBIs and 137 runs scored. He also collected 212 hits, including 51 doubles. He edged out Colorado's Todd Helton to win the NL batting title, becoming at age 23 the youngest batting champion in the league since the Dodgers' Tommy Davis led the league in 1962, when he was also 23.

AP/WWP

Albert's totals led the major leagues in runs scored, doubles, extra-base hits and total bases. He became only the second player in Cardinal history to hit 40 homers and collect 200 hits in the same season, a feat previously accomplished only by Rogers Hornsby in 1922.

"As a pitcher, you know if you make a mistake he's going to make you pay for it," said the Marlins' Chad Fox. "But he can still find a way to produce with your best pitch. That's intimidating."

Albert's .359 average was the best by a Cardinal since Joe Torre hit .363 in 1971; His 212 hits were the most by a Cardinal since Willie McGee had 216 in 1985; his 137 runs scored were the most by a Cardinal since Hornsby scored 141 in 1922; and his 51 doubles was the highest total by a Cardinal since Musial had 53 in 1953.

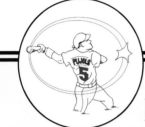

Did you know...?

In 2003, Albert became the youngest batting champion in the National League since Tommy Davis of the Dodgers in 1962. Both were 23 years old. In a vote by major league players, Albert was awarded the Players' Choice Major League Player of the Year award as well as the National League's Outstanding Player trophy.

RIGHT: Albert's intensity at the plate carries over to his time spent off the field studying his at-bats and analyzing opposing pitchers.

Yet another indication that he was becoming an even better hitter, if that was possible, was that he struck out only 65 times in 685 plate appearances.

One of the highlights of his season was a 30-game hitting streak, the longest by a Cardinal since Musial hit in 30 consecutive games in 1950. He fell three games shy of the team-record 33-game streak set by Hornsby in 1922.

Albert was impressed with that accomplishment.

"You're talking about Hall of Famers," he said. "I think it's great when they throw your name out there with the longest Cardinal hitting streaks. You got your name out there with Stan Musial, the best hitter to ever pass through the Cardinal organization."

He might have been able to break that record if not for a case of the flu that

hit him just as he extended the streak to 30 games. He missed the next four games, then went zero for five in his first game back.

His performance for the year again earned Albert a second-place finish behind Bonds in the MVP voting, and his totals for the first three years of his career put him in a category reserved for the best players in the history of the game.

Albert tied Ralph Kiner for the record of hitting the most homers in the first three seasons in the majors, at 114. He became only the third player to hit 30 or more homers in the first three years of his career, joining Mark McGwire and Jose Canseco. He became the only player in history to hit 30 homers, drive in 100 runs and score 100 runs in each of his first three seasons.

Bonds, who had earlier been skeptical of Albert's success, saying he did not really have a regular position because

"You're talking about Hall of Famers.

You got your name out there with

Stan Musial, the best hitter to ever

(A L B E R T   P U J O L S)

pass through the Cardinal organization."

he shifted between so many positions during his first two seasons, could not make that same claim in 2003 when Albert played 113 games in left field and 36 at first base. Instead, Bonds chose to criticize Albert by saying that the true test of how great a player he was would be proven by longevity and by his total production over the length of his career.

"Who does he compare to?" Bonds repeated a question. "Alex Rodriguez, Ken Griffey Jr., those types of players. It took me a little while longer. I played a couple extra years before I understood the game. They learned it a lot faster than I did, within about a three-year span.

"Give Pujols time. I tell people a story about a kid who's been like my brother for-ever in this game of baseball, and happens to have had a lot of injuries, and no one

ever talks about Junior (Griffey) anymore. So before you put Pujols on that pedestal, let him play for a while first, because he's not there yet."

Many would disagree with Bonds and form a different opinion about Albert's accomplishments and success. Despite Albert's personal success, however, the Cardinals' collective season was a disappointment as their three-year run of playoff appearances came to an end. The team finished in third place in the NL Central with an 85-77 record, three games behind the champion Chicago Cubs.

For a player as team-oriented as Albert, that was really the only statistic from the season that mattered. He could not wait for the 2004 season to begin, to get another chance to try to lead the Cardinals to the N.L. championship and the team's first trip back to the World Series after a 17-year drought.

DILIP VISHWANAT/GETTY IMAGES

Albert the Great: The Albert Pujols Story

A Banner Season

By the start of the 2004 season, Albert had not only placed his name in baseball's record book, but he also had established himself as one of the best players in the game—regardless of age.

He even had his mug and his name on the cover of a popular baseball video game.

Then, shortly before the season began, he signed his name to a seven-year, $100 million contract that runs through 2010 with an option for 2011. The contract afforded him the title of "richest player in the storied history of the Cardinals."

The pressure of trying to prove he was worthy of that contract affected Albert at the beginning of the season even though he tried to downplay his slow start. He hit "only" .287 in April with seven homers and 17 RBIs. It was the first month he hit less than .300 since June 2002.

The Cardinals, picked by most observers to finish third in the division behind the Cubs and Astros, got off to a sluggish start as well, finishing May with a 27-23 record. But both Albert and his teammates were about to go on a streak that would launch them toward one of the best seasons in team history.

Between June 1 and the All-Star break, the Cardinals won 27 of 37 games and built a seven-game lead in their division. That was only a small indication of the success that was to come the remainder of the year.

The Cardinals went a collective 41-12 in July and August, blowing away the rest of the division, and nobody was more responsible for that success than Albert. He hit .374 with nine homers and 22 RBIs in 24 games in July, and in August hit .351 with 12 homers and 29 RBIs in 27 games.

On July 20 in Chicago, Albert enjoyed one of the best games of his career as he hit three homers and drove in five runs against the Cubs. In the game, the Cardinals climbed back from deficits of 7-1 and 8-2, eventually winning 11-8 on Albert's tie-breaking ninth-inning homer. It was the first three-homer game by a Cardinal since Mark McGwire in 2000.

What impressed La Russa more than the individual performance, however, was the fact that Albert was putting the team and a desire to win above his personal accomplishments.

RIGHT: In 2004, at the request of St. Louis general manager Walt Jocketty, Albert became the Cardinals' first 100-million dollar man.

"The true winning player lets the

numbers, the stats and the money

(T O N Y   L A   R U S S A)

happen. That's what he does."

AP/WWP

"The best thing about Albert is he's playing to win," La Russa said. "He's playing for a ring for himself, his teammates and the Cardinals fans. That's what I admire about him most. Nothing else is a close second. The true winning player lets the numbers, the stats and the money happen. That's what he does."

Albert did at least get personal about one issue in the middle of the season. Despite finishing second in the Home Run Derby at the All-Star game in 2003, he was not one of the initial players invited to participate the night before the game in Houston. When injuries and cancellations created openings later, Albert was asked and politely declined.

He did play in the game, collecting his first two hits in All-Star competition, both doubles, but the N.L. lost the game. The outcome seemed uneventful at the time, but would prove significant a little

Did you know...?

In 2004, eight of Albert's last nine hits of the regular season were doubles, increasing his season total of doubles to 51 for the second consecutive year. He became the first Cardinal to reach 50 doubles in consecutive years since Joe Medwick in 1936-37.

LEFT: Despite getting off to a slow, frustrating start in 2004, both Albert Pujols and the Cardinals turned it on as the summer heated up.

over three months later when it came time to determine which league would have home-field advantage for the World Series.

The Cardinals' big lead in the division could have afforded the team the chance to think far in advance—but they didn't. Albert and teammates were more concerned with continuing to push and win games one day at a time rather than looking too much at the big picture.

Such was the case on August 3, playing at home against Montreal, when Albert connected in the first inning for his 30th homer of the season. That homer established him as the only player in baseball history to hit 30 or more homers in each of the first four years of his career.

Albert's reaction was expected.

"I'm glad I'm the only guy, but there's still a lot of the season left," he said. "I just want to stay consistent. It's just a home run."

Said La Russa after the game, "He's the only guy in history, that's how special it is. It's got to be pretty hard, really hard, if nobody's ever done it."

What made that homer even more impressive is that he reached the 30-homer plateau before he recorded his 30th strikeout of the season.

"He's a smarter hitter," La Russa said. "He's had three and a half great years. ... People are more aware of him. To maintain what you're doing, you've got to improve.

"He really trusts his hands. When you do that, you wait longer, you don't try to overswing. A lot of his success [comes from the fact that] he doesn't overcommit to anything. He just sees [the ball] and trusts his hands. It's a great way to do it."

Not only did the homer ensure that Albert was the first player to hit 30 or more homers in his first four years in the majors, it also made him the only hitter in Cardinals history—at any point in their careers—to hit 30 or more homers in four consecutive years.

But Albert's season wasn't done. On August 29, at Pittsburgh, he blasted his 40th homer of the year, a hit that also drove in his 100th run of the season.

It was the second consecutive 40-homer season for Albert and his fourth 100-RBI year in a row, again putting him in the company of baseball greats. The only other players to drive in 100 or more runs their first four years in the majors were Al Simmons, Ted Williams and Joe DiMaggio.

"That's about as good as it gets," La Russa said.

Added Albert, "It's awesome. Forty and 100 is tough to do at this level, but I don't care what kind of numbers I put up or who they compare me to. I just want to be a winner.

"When you start thinking about your numbers and what you've done in the big leagues, that's when you start feeling comfortable, and I don't want to do that."

One of his former teammates who continued to be amazed by Albert's performance was McGwire.

"He's an intimidating figure at the plate," McGwire said. "He's got that sense of 'You're never going to get me out,' which all the great players have. In the future, it's going to be him and A-Rod (Alex Rodriguez). They're superstars now. But talk to me in 10 years and it's going to be crazy to see what those guys have done."

Albert reached another personal milestone before the season ended. On September 26 at Colorado, he surpassed the 500-RBI mark for his young career. He became the first player in 62 years to record that many RBIs in his first four seasons in the majors, joining Williams and DiMaggio.

"I'm taking one year at a time, and the last four years have been great," he said.

RIGHT: Albert finally found a home on defense in 2004: first base.

"He's an intimidating figure at the plate.

He's got that sense of 'You're never

going to get me out,' which all the

(M A R K   M c G W I R E)

great players have."

For the first time in his short career, Albert benefited from spending the entire season at one position, first base, which most observers consider his most natural and best position. The trade of Tino Martinez to Tampa Bay over the winter opened up the spot, and Albert made the most of the move. His defense proved to be outstanding, with some people even predicting he could one day win a Gold Glove.

What was missing from the previous three seasons of Albert's career was a chance to earn the elusive ring that goes to members of the World Championship team. As the Cardinals headed into the postseason on the strength of a 105-win season, the second highest win total in the history of the franchise, many thought this would be his chance to fulfill that dream.

ABOVE: Albert watches another homer sail over the fence. The slugger had 46 moments like this in 2004 as he reached his peak for home runs in a season.

Albert the Great: The Albert Pujols Story

A Trip to the Series

CHAPTER NINE

Playing in the playoffs was not a new experience for Albert, who made his third trip to the postseason in his four-year career in 2004. The difference this time was that he was established as the Cardinals' star, and the team itself was "the team to beat."

The first-round opponent was the Los Angeles Dodgers, champions of the N.L. West. Albert made certain the series got off to a positive start for the Cardinals by

homering off Odalis Perez in his first at-bat in the first inning. He also singled and scored in a five-run third inning that blew the game open and sent the Cardinals to the 8-3 victory. After the Cardinals won by the same score the following night, the series headed west to Los Angeles with the Cardinals leading the best-of-five series two games to none.

Jose Lima shut out the Cardinals in the third game, but it was Albert's home

ABOVE: Albert is drenched in champagne by
teammates after the Cardinals clinched the
2004 NLDS with a 6-2 win over the Dodgers.

AP/WWP

"When you take things for granted, that's when it slips away from you. We don't want that to happen."

(A L B E R T   P U J O L S)

run in Game 4 that lifted St. Louis back into the NLCS for the second time in three seasons. The Cardinals lost to the Giants in 2002, and Albert wanted a different outcome in the 2004 series against the Houston Astros.

As he had done in his first at-bat in the first game of the division series, Albert jumped on a pitch from Brandon Backe in the first inning of Game 1 for a two-run homer. The homer wiped out a short-lived 2-0 lead by Houston, and the Cardinals went on to a 10-7 victory.

He waited longer for his heroic feat in Game 2, settling for two singles and a run scored before he came to bat in the eighth inning with the score tied 4-4. He greeted reliever Dan Miceli with a home run, and when Scott Rolen followed with another homer, it marked the first time in Cardinals postseason history that they had hit back-to-back homers. The two blasts gave St.

Louis a 6-4 win and a 2-0 series lead going to Houston.

The Cardinals were confident they could close out the Astros during the three games in Houston, but the Astros—who had lost only once at home in more than a month—had other ideas. Albert did homer in Game 4, but the Astros won all three games in Houston to send the series back to St. Louis with the Cardinals trailing three games to two.

Carlos Beltran and Lance Berkman of the Astros were battling with Albert for status as the hottest hitter in the series, and they combined for a first-inning run for Houston in Game 6. It was the first time all season the Cardinals had played a potential elimination game.

In the bottom of the first, Albert stepped to the plate against Pete Munro with Tony Womack on second. He blasted his sixth homer of the postseason, and fourth of the series, to put the Cardinals ahead 2-1. Albert's leadoff double in his next at-bat in the third ignited a two-run rally that put the Cardinals ahead 4-2, but the Astros came back and tied the game in the ninth, sending it to extra innings. The tie lasted until the 12th inning, when Albert earned a leadoff walk from Miceli, and one out later teammate Jim Edmonds slammed a two-run walkoff homer that gave the Cardinals the win and forced a seventh and deciding game.

In the postgame news conference, Albert said the win was typical of the way the Cardinals' entire season had gone, that the team was always determined and never wanted to give up.

"When you take things for granted, that's when it slips away from you," Albert said. "We don't want that to happen. We don't want to wait until next year. One hundred sixty-two games and wait and see if we're going to be in this situation. There's one game away to get us to the next level. We're going to try to make it happen."

Waiting on the mound for the decisive Game 7 was Hall of Famer-to-be Roger Clemens. If the Cardinals were lucky enough to get past Clemens, Astros closer Brad Lidge, who had been dominant during the series, would get the ball.

Lidge, for one, knew what was waiting for Houston, too, the hot bat of Albert Pujols.

"I'll tell you what," Lidge said. "I've never seen a hitter as strong as he is."

RIGHT: Albert celebrates as he scores the go-ahead run in the seventh game of the NLCS on Scott Rolen's two-run homer off Roger Clemens.

Did you know...?

After signing a seven-year, $100 million contract in February 2004, Albert said he would donate money toward building a baseball stadium in his native Dominican Republic.

Albert just missed hitting a game-tying homer off Lidge in the ninth inning of Game 4 in Houston, coming up just a few feet short of the left field wall.

"The last pitch he actually hit with one hand," Lidge said. "It was kind of in the dirt, and he pushed it back to the warning track. He's a premier power hitter."

What impressed Albert's manager, as had been the case all season and throughout his career, was his intensity and drive to be successful. He wasn't expecting anything less heading into Game 7.

"He's playing like a man possessed because he wants to win a league championship and go to the next level," La Russa said. "He's got a bunch of teammates who are playing the same way. He's into it."

Added Albert: "There's no hero. Everybody, we know what we need to do to get ready. If one guy fails, then the other guy knows he has to pick it up. That's why we've been so successful during the year and in the playoffs."

The formula would hold true for one more magical night. With Clemens and the Astros 10 outs away from eliminating the Cardinals and reaching the World Series for the first time in franchise history, Albert stepped to the plate in the sixth inning with St. Louis losing 2-1.

Roger Cedeno, the tying run, was on third. Albert was two for 14 lifetime against Clemens, including zero for five in the series, during which he was 12 for 21 against the rest of the

Houston pitchers. Manager Phil Garner trotted out to discuss the situation with Clemens and catcher Brad Ausmus.

The decision was made to challenge Albert. Clemens threw three fastballs, and worked the count to 1-2.

"With two strikes, even Albert Pujols is not as good a hitter," Ausmus said. "We were going with a two-seamer, down and in, but Roger got it just a little bit up."

Albert sent the pitch into the left field corner for a double that scored Cedeno to tie the game. As Albert stood on second, he knew it was a moment he would remember forever.

"I'm going to keep dreaming about it for the next couple of weeks," Albert said. "I didn't want to try to do too much, just see a good pitch to hit. He didn't make a bad pitch, just thank the Lord my hands came through."

Clemens didn't have much time to mope, just as Albert didn't have much time to celebrate. On Clemens's next pitch, Scott Rolen slammed a two-run homer over the left field wall that sent the Cardinals to a 6-4 victory and onto the World Series.

"This is what you dream about, going to the World Series, as a little boy," Albert said. "Getting the opportunity to play Game 7 against the best pitcher in baseball for the past 20 years, Roger Clemens, he's amazing. It doesn't get any better than that."

Albert was named the MVP of the playoff series after hitting .500 (14 for 28 with four homers and nine RBIs); his 14 hits marked the most hits recorded in a seven-game postseason series.

"Everyone in this locker room is the MVP," Albert said. "That's why the trophy will be staying in the locker room for the rest of my career."

The Cardinals, of course, had no way of knowing it would be the last time they would celebrate a victory in 2004. Their opponent in the World Series, the wild-card Boston Red Sox, had destiny on their side and that became too formidable an opponent for Albert and company.

The series opened in Boston, who had been given home-field advantage due to the American League's victory in the All-Star game, and the Cardinals failed to take advantage of four Red Sox errors in losing the opener 11-9. It became the only game they really had a chance to win. The Red Sox won Game 2, 6-2, leaving St. Louis down 2-0 as the series returned to Busch Stadium.

The deficit still did not discourage the Cardinals or their fans, who knew the team was a perfect 6-0 in postseason home games. A 4-1 loss in Game 3, however, was a major letdown, and the Red Sox completed the sweep with a 3-0 victory in Game 4. The Red Sox became the fourth team in history to sweep the World Series and never trail at any point in the four games.

The Cardinals' offense, which had been so formidable during the regular season and NL playoffs, disappeared against the Red Sox. The third-, fourth- and fifth-place hitters in the St. Louis lineup—Albert, Rolen and Edmonds—combined to go six for 45 in the series, and Albert had five of the six hits. Rolen was zero for 15, and Edmonds's only hit was a bunt single. Rolen had the trio's lone RBI,

coming on a sacrifice fly. As a team the Cardinals hit only .190 against Boston, a fact that almost nobody could explain.

Still, Albert and teammates were quick to congratulate the Red Sox for winning their first world championship since 1918, and to realize that when the pain of that loss fades away, they still will have plenty of memories from an unbelievable season.

"It seemed like everything was going their way," Albert said in a quiet St. Louis locker room after the final loss of the series. "But we had a great year. I'm proud of the way we battled. It didn't finish like we wanted, it just didn't happen.

"We were the second best team, and nobody expected us to get this far. Somebody is going to win the World Series, and it just wasn't us.

"Now we've got to just prepare ourselves for next year."

As he has throughout his career, Albert will rely on his faith in God and his family to help him do that.

AP/WWP

ABOVE: Albert makes a difficult play in the field to force out Red Sox runner Bill Mueller at home in Game 4 of the World Series.

Faith and Family

CHAPTER TEN

Albert does not believe any of the success he has achieved in baseball would have been possible without his strong faith in God and the love and support of his wife, Deidre. His love and devotion to baseball rank third on his list, behind God and his family.

"I try to spend as much time as possible with God and my family," Albert said. "That's more important than anything I am doing in baseball."

Adds his wife, Deidre: "Albert's source for everything in life, for being the man he is, for being the baseball player he is, the dad and the husband, [is God]. If it wasn't for that, he might not be where he is."

Albert was an 18-year-old senior at Fort Osage High School when he went out one night to Cashmere, a Latin dance club in Kansas City. Deidre, also known as Dee-Dee, was there too. The couple ended up

Albert the Great: The Albert Pujols Story

"I try to spend as much time as

possible with God and my family.

That's more important than

(A L B E R T   P U J O L S)

anything I am doing in baseball."

RIGHT: Albert is never shy about giving credit or showing thanks to God for helping him become a major-leaguer.

dancing and having a good time even though she spoke no Spanish and he spoke very little English. Albert said he was the same age as she was, 21, which was the minimum age required for admission to the club.

Albert eventually worked up the nerve to ask for her phone number, and asked her out on a date. There, he said he had a confession to make—that he had lied about his age.

Deidre asked him if he was 22 instead, or maybe 23. When he said he was 18, she was stunned. "You're barely legal," she said.

Deidre had grown up in the Kansas City area and had already graduated from college at Kansas State and was working as a secretary. She wasn't sure she wanted to get seriously involved with Albert, but she told him she had a confession to make, too—she was

a single mother with a daughter, Isabella, who was eight weeks old.

The news didn't affect Albert's interest in her, so a week later Deidre gave him the rest of her news— Isabella had been born with Down Syndrome.

Deidre didn't want her daughter's condition to be misinterpreted by Albert, who was still learning English, so she gave him Spanish-language pamphlets about the disorder. When he finally met her, Albert said he immediately viewed himself as her dad.

The couple stayed together after Albert graduated early from high school, and Albert cared for Isabella while Deidre was at work. Despite their different backgrounds and heritages, the couple discovered they had much in common. When she had been a senior in high school, Deidre was part of a group of Kansas City area students who traveled to Central America to work in impoverished communities. She benefited from a very stable home life, far different than Albert's early childhood.

"My parents were together and supported me in everything," Deidre said. "I know what family values are. Albert grew up in the Dominican Republic with no mom, his dad going off a lot for long periods of time to work, so his grandma and grandpa were the ones there for him.

"There was always movement in Albert's life, not the secure home that I think a child needs. I'm really amazed that Albert came out of that with really strong family values."

The couple married on New Year's Day 2000, so Albert wouldn't forget the date, Deidre said. They soon added another member to their family, son A.J.

Almost from the moment he met Isabella, Albert began working to help raise money for and awareness of Down Syndrome. Before a game in September 2002, a 10-year-old girl with Down Syndrome, Kathleen Mertz of Lake Saint Louis, Missouri, threw out the ceremonial first pitch. Albert was the catcher and he signed her shirt while they talked.

"I could see her talking to him, and she was acting like she was swinging the bat," Tracey Mertz, Kathleen's mother, told the St. Louis Post-Dispatch. "She yelled, 'Hey Albert, hit me a home run.'" Albert smiled and nodded.

In the first inning, with two runners on base, Albert delivered a three-run homer.

Albert did not forget about the girl after the game. Seven months later, in April 2003, he served as an honorary chairman of a golf tournament and auction for the benefit of the Down Syndrome Association of St. Louis. NFL player Andy McCollum was the other honorary chairman.

Mrs. Mertz was one of the fundraiser's organizers, and Kathleen was there, wearing her Albert Pujols jersey.

RIGHT: Deidre Pujols has always shared in Albert's success. Here, she celebrates with him after the Cardinals advanced to the NLCS in 2004.

"There was always movement in

Albert's life, not the secure home

that I think a child needs. I'm really

(D E I D R E   P U J O L S)

amazed that Albert came out of that

with really strong family values."

RIGHT: Albert passes along some of
his hitting secrets to his son A.J.
during spring training in 2004.

Kathleen was asked to speak to the audience.

"Hello, my name is Kathleen Mertz," she said. "I am in the fourth grade at Green Tree Elementary. Did you know I got 100 percent on my states and capitals test? I made the honor roll. My parents are very proud. I am 10 years old and guess what? Tomorrow is my birthday. I have a special birthday wish. I would love to get my pic- ture taken with my favorite football and baseball players, Andy and Albert. Do you think my wish will come true? Thanks for playing golf today. I hope you had fun."

The auction followed, and Albert decided to give Kathleen another birthday present. He had the winning bid of $3,000 for a trip for four to Orlando, Florida, including air fare, hotel accommodations, car rental and

AP/WWP

VIP passes to Sea World or Busch Gardens. Albert then gave the trip to Kathleen and her family.

Later in the auction, Albert bought another trip to Florida for the same price of $3,000 and donated it to another Down Syndrome child and his family.

Albert knows how much his life has been touched by having a child with Down Syndrome, a feeling Kathleen's mother understands as well.

"When I had Kathleen, I never imagined all of the wonderful things that would happen to us," Mrs. Mertz told the *Post-Dispatch*. "It's an incredible journey through the world with these kids. I didn't even know who I was until she was born."

How Good
Can He Be?

CHAPTER ELEVEN

The ultimate question about Albert Pujols does not concern any of his great accomplishments to this point in his career. It is the question about what will happen in the future. How good can he be?

Another hitter who already is about to re-write history, again, thinks Albert has a chance to become one of the all-time best.

"If he plays for a long period of time, he definitely has a chance to do some wonderful things in this game because he has the ability," said the Giants' Barry Bonds. "It's just time that dictates what happens."

Many longtime observers already say Albert has established himself as the best player on the Cardinals since Stan Musial. Others say he might have the best

"If he plays for a long period of time,

he definitely has a chance to do some

wonderful things in this game because

(BARRY BONDS)

he has the ability. It's just time

that dictates what happens."

LEFT: Albert watches another home run sail into the stands during the 2003 Home Run Derby at the All-Star game.

chance of any current player in the majors to win the Triple Crown, which has not been accomplished in either league since Boston's Carl Yastrzemski did it in 1967. No National Leaguer has completed the feat since the Cardinals' Joe Medwick in 1937. In the Triple Crown categories in the National League in 2004, Albert finished fifth in batting average with a .331 mark; second in home runs with 46 and third in RBIs with 123. The only other hitter in the top 10 in all three categories was the Dodgers' Adrian Beltre.

Others say Albert might be the best bet to become the first hitter since Ted Williams in 1941 to hit .400 for a season. His career high average was the league-leading mark of .359 in 2003. One attribute that Albert has working in his favor in his pursuit of .400 and the batting title is his ability to put the ball in play and his disciplined eye at the plate. His strikeout total has decreased each of his four years in the majors, down to 52 in 692 plate appearances in 2004.

At the same time, his walk total has increased each of his four seasons, up to 84 in 2004.

Trying to accomplish either is not a driving force in Albert's basebal life.

"I really don't care about my average as long as I produce runs," he said. "How much difference is there between hitting .380, .370 or .330 if you're helping your club? I think about having quality at-bats, that's all."

La Russa is worried about all of the distractions that might bother Albert if he is ever in a serious position to challenge for hitting .400 or winning the Triple Crown. He saw what happened as McGwire was tracking down Roger Maris's home run record in 1998.

"I think he can handle it," La Russa said. "But everyone wants to be around it when someone does something special. I watched it with Mark. He had to really work at keeping his focus."

One person who thinks Albert can do it is his former hitting coach with the Cardinals, Mitchell Page, who worked with Albert from 2000-2004.

"He's got all the ability in the world to be the next Triple Crown hitter," Page said. "If he's close in September, the way he goes about his game and knows what he wants to do ... I'll bet everything that he'll win the Triple Crown if he's that close."

With or without a Triple Crown or a .400 batting average, Albert still can be expected to post some of the best offensive numbers ever if he continues to hit at his current pace.

When he attended the fourth game of the 2003 World Series, Albert had a chance to meet and talk with Hank Aaron, baseball's all-time home run hitter. He did not waste that opportunity to learn from the Hall of Famer.

"I asked him about when he was young and all that stuff," Albert said. "He played this game for 23 years, and he never hit more than 47 home runs (in a season). He had 755 home runs. I just wish that when I'm done, I have half the home runs he's got."

That might prove to be a great underestimation by Albert. However his career concludes, Albert knows he will be extremely grateful and thankful to God for the opportunity to play in the major leagues.

"I know I've never taken anything for granted," he said. "I wanted to make it to the big leagues, where I am today. I thank God for the opportunity and the talent He gave me. You have to have talent, but you have to dedicate yourself and work hard. There are a lot of guys who have talent who don't want to work hard.

"When I walk out of this game 15 years or so from now, I want to be the best player I can be. I want to be remembered as a dedicated worker who never got lazy. I want to be the same Albert Pujols a year from now. I want to be the same person no matter how much success I might have."

ABOVE: Albert is presented with the NL Hank Aaron
Award at the World Series in 2003 by Hank Aaron.

"He's smooth through the zone. With guys like that, that means they're waiting a little longer, and they've got the strength to wait. You've got to admire the way he's disciplined (at the plate) at such a very young age."

(Atlanta manager Bobby Cox)

"He has a great instinct for the game, whether it's running the bases or adjusting to the pitchers or playing different positions. He's one of those guys who is just gifted."

(Cardinals general manager Walt Jocketty)

"You'll hear what he has to say in a meeting, then watch him go out a couple hours later and execute it perfectly. Everyone can see his ability. But he has insight way beyond his years."

(Former Cardinals catcher Mike Matheny)

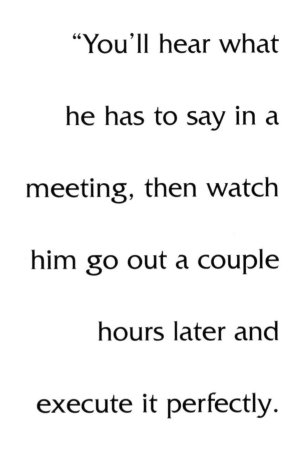

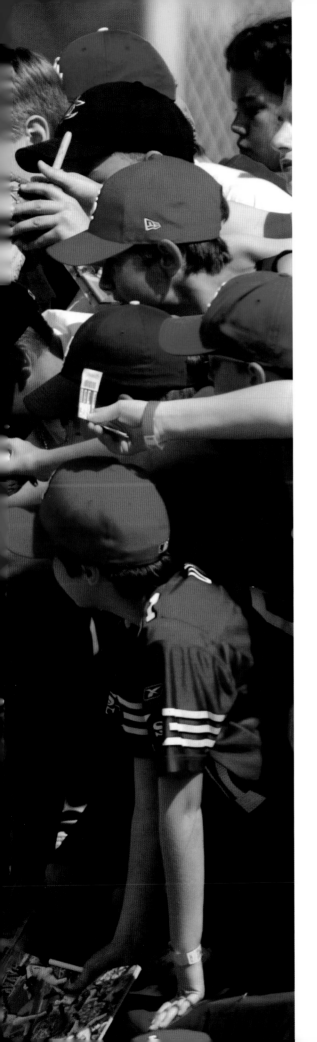

"He signed a big

contract and hasn't

let up at all. He's

trying to find ways

to get better."

(Cardinals general
manager
Walt Jocketty)

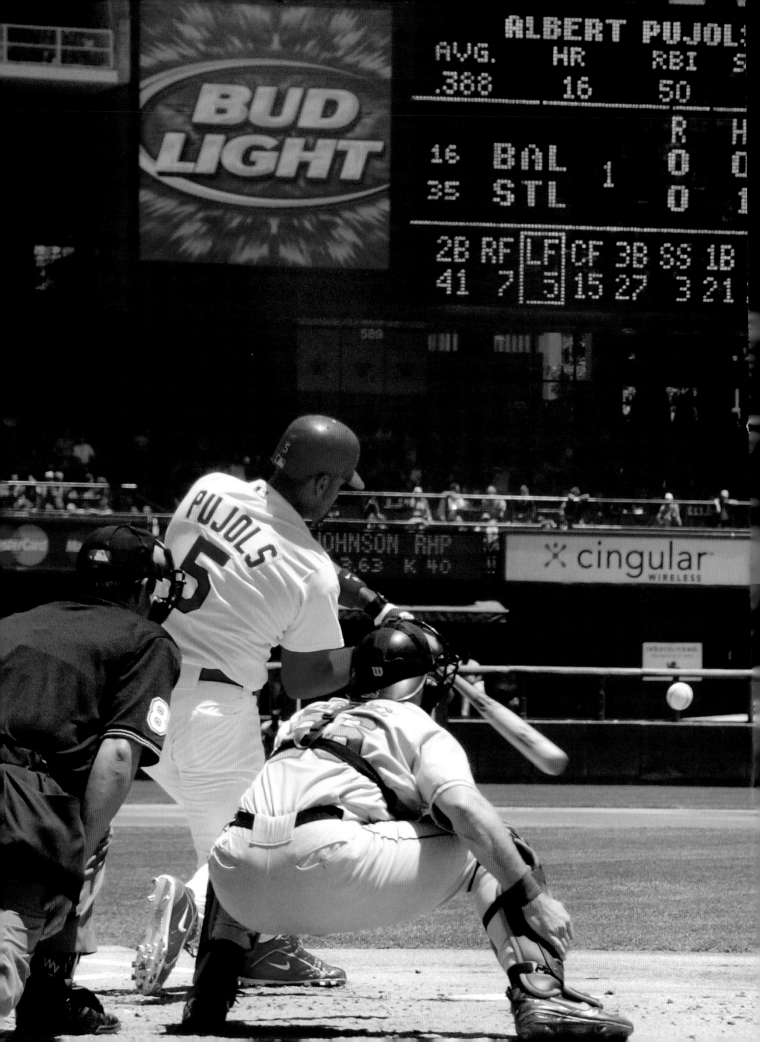

"He can beat you

with the bat so bad.

He's one of the best

hitters in baseball. ...

It seems every chance

he gets, he puts the

ball to the wall."

(Outfielder
Carlos Beltran)

"The stuff this guy does, the quality at-bats, the pitches he does things with ... I mean, it's up there with the great players."

(Cardinals manager Tony La Russa)

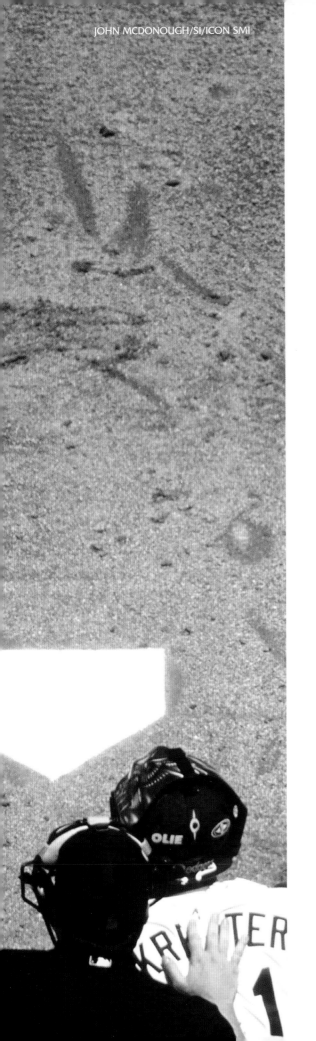

"He has an obsession with hitting. And you know what? The real good hitters all have an obsession with hitting. He's a force. He's got no weaknesses."

(Tampa Bay manager Lou Piniella)

Career Stats 2001-2004

Regular Season

YEAR	G	AB	R	H	2B	3B	HR	RBI	BB	SO	BA	OBP	SLG	Total Bases
2001	161	590	112	194	47	4	37	130	69	93	.329	.403	.610	360
2002	157	590	118	185	40	2	34	127	72	69	.314	.394	.561	331
2003	157	591	137	212	51	1	43	124	79	65	.359	.439	.667	394
2004	154	592	133	196	51	2	46	123	84	52	.331	.415	.657	389
TOTALS	629	2363	500	787	189	9	160	504	304	279	.333	.413	.624	1474

Postseason

YEAR	G	AB	R	H	2B	3B	HR	RBI	BB	SO	BA	OBP	SLG	Total Bases
2001	5	18	1	2	0	0	1	2	2	2	.111	.200	.278	5
2002	8	29	5	8	1	1	1	5	5	6	.276	.400	.483	14
2004	15	58	15	24	4	0	6	14	8	6	.414	.493	.793	46
TOTALS	28	105	21	34	5	1	8	21	15	14	.324	.418	.619	65

Career Home Runs 2001-2004

2001

No.	Date	Opponent	Pitcher	No.	Date	Opponent	Pitcher
1	April 6	at Arizona	Reynoso	20	June 12	at Kansas City	Durbin
2	April 9	Colorado	Neagle	21	June 26	Cincinnati	Nichting
3	April 12	Colorado	Hampton	22	July 14	Detroit	Lima
4	April 14	Houston	Elarton	23	July 18	at Houston	Oswalt
5	April 22	at Houston	Miller	24	July 25	Houston	Redding
6	April 22	at Houston	Miller	25	July 28	at Chicago	Wood
7	April 25	Montreal	Reames	26	Aug. 4	Florida	Burnett
8	April 28	New York	Franco	27	Aug. 7	at Montreal	Vasquez
9	May 6	at Atlanta	Millwood	28	Aug. 12	at New York	Chen
10	May 7	Pittsburgh	Ritchie	29	Aug. 20	at Cincinnati	Reitsma
11	May 10	Pittsburgh	Manzanillo	30	Aug. 23	at Cincinnati	Dessens
12	May 12	Chicago	Farnsworth	31	Aug. 29	San Diego	Lundquist
13	May 13	Chicago	Heredia	32	Sept. 3	at San Diego	B. Jones
14	May 15	at Pittsburgh	Olivares	33	Sept. 4	at San Diego	Jodie
15	May 28	Milwaukee	Rigdon	34	Sept. 5	at San Diego	Jarvis
16	May 28	Milwaukee	King	35	Sept. 18	Milwaukee	Wright
17	June 8	at Colorado	Neagle	36	Sept. 21	at Pittsburgh	Olivares
18	June 9	at Colorado	Astacio	37	Sept. 30	Pittsburgh	McKnight
19	June 10	at Colorado	Hampton				

2002

No.	Date	Opponent	Pitcher	No.	Date	Opponent	Pitcher
38	April 6	at Houston	Hernandez	55	July 2	San Diego	Jarvis
39	April 16	at Arizona	Johnson	56	July 4	Los Angeles	Ishii
40	April 19	at Milwaukee	Quevedo	57	July 5	Los Angeles	O. Perez
41	April 23	at New York	D'Amico	58	July 7	Los Angeles	Carrara
42	April 24	at New York	Weathers	59	July 17	San Francisco	Hernandez
43	May 17	Cincinnati	Dessens	60	July 21	at Pittsburgh	Fogg
44	May 20	Cincinnati	Haynes	61	Aug. 8	Montreal	Reames
45	May 25	at Pittsburgh	Anderson	62	Aug. 10	New York	Estes
46	May 26	at Pittsburgh	Fogg	63	Aug. 12	at Pittsburgh	Boehringer
47	May 28	at Houston	Reynolds	64	Aug. 14	at Pittsburgh	Sauerbeck
48	June 2	Pittsburgh	Benson	65	Aug. 15	at Pittsburgh	Benson
49	June 4	at Cincinnati	Hamilton	66	Aug. 19	Pittsburgh	Wells
50	June 8	at Kansas City	Suzuki	67	Aug. 27 (1)	at Cincinnati	Moehler
51	June 11	at Seattle	Baldwin	68	Aug. 30	at Chicago	Zambrano
52	June 19	Anaheim	Sele	69	Aug. 31 (1)	at Chicago	Prior
53	June 23	at Chicago	Wood	70	Sept. 19	at Colorado	T. Jones
54	July 1	San Diego	Perez	71	Sept. 22	Houston	Saarloos

Career Home Runs 2001-2004

2003

No.	Date	Opponent	Pitcher	No.	Date	Opponent	Pitcher
72	April 3	Milwaukee	Kinney	94	June 29	at Kansas City	George
73	April 4	Houston	Moehler	95	July 3	San Francisco	Rueter
74	April 25	at Florida	Burnett	96	July 4	at Chicago	Wood
75	April 30	New York	Astacio	97	July 5	at Chicago	Estes
76	April 30	New York	Astacio	98	July 12	San Diego	Herges
77	May 3	Montreal	Vargas	99	July 18	at Los Angeles	Ishii
78	May 6	at Cincinnati	White	100	July 20	at Los Angeles	O. Perez
79	May 8	at Cincinnati	Wilson	101	Aug. 2	at New York	Seo
80	May 13	Cincinnati	Wilson	102	Aug. 10	Atlanta	Smoltz
81	May 17	Chicago	Prior	103	Aug. 11	at Pittsburgh	Wells
82	May 19	Chicago	Farnsworth	104	Aug. 12	at Pittsburgh	Fogg
83	May 20	at Houston	Miller	105	Aug. 13	at Pittsburgh	Meadows
84	May 21	at Houston	Munro	106	Aug. 26	Chicago	Prior
85	May 22	at Houston	Robertson	107	Aug. 31	at Cincinnati	Serafini
86	May 31	Pittsburgh	Wells	108	Aug. 31	at Cincinnati	Graves
87	June 5	Toronto	Towers	109	Sept. 5	Cincinnati	Harang
88	June 10	at Boston	Seanez	110	Sept. 6	Cincinnati	Serafini
89	June 15	at New York (AL)	Mussina	111	Sept. 10	Colorado	Elarton
90	June 17	at Milwaukee	Kinney	112	Sept. 10	Colorado	Bernero
91	June 19	at Milwaukee	Quevedo	113	Sept. 15	Milwaukee	Rusch
92	June 21	Kansas City	Buckvich	114	Sept. 20	Houston	Miceli
93	June 29	at Kansas City	George				

Career Home Run Breakdown By Opponent

Cincinnati	21	Florida	3
Pittsburgh	21	San Francisco	3
Chicago (NL)	19	Seattle	2
Houston	18	Anaheim	1
Colorado	11	Boston	1
Milwaukee	11	Detroit	1
San Diego	10	New York (AL)	1
New York (NL)	9	Toronto	1
Montreal	7		
Atlanta	6		
Kansas City	5		
Los Angeles	5		
Arizona	4		

Career Grand Slams

Date	Opponent	Pitcher
Sept. 21, 2001	at Pittsburgh	Olivares
June 11, 2002	at Seattle	Baldwin
Aug. 10, 2002	New York	Estes

Career Walkoff Home Runs

Date	Opponent	Pitcher
July 12, 2003	San Diego	Herges
Sept. 20, 2003	Houston	Miceli
June 18, 2004	Cincinnati	Matthews
Aug. 4, 2004	Montreal	Cordero

Career Home Runs 2001-2004

2004

No.	Date	Opponent	Pitcher	No.	Date	Opponent	Pitcher
115	April 8	Milwaukee	Capuano	138	July 17	at Cincinnati	Jones
116	April 8	Milwaukee	Burba	139	July 20	at Chicago	Rusch
117	April 9	at Arizona	Daigle	140	July 20	at Chicago	Farnsworth
118	April 11	at Arizona	Johnson	141	July 20	at Chicago	Hawkins
119	April 17	Colorado	Estes	142	July 23	San Francisco	Hermanson
120	April 20	at Houston	Miller	143	July 26	at Cincinnati	Wilson
121	April 25	at Milwaukee	Sheets	144	Aug. 3	Montreal	Kim
122	May 3	Chicago	Maddux	145	Aug. 4	Montreal	Cordero
123	May 9	at Montreal	Vargas	146	Aug. 10	at Florida	Beckett
124	May 20	at New York	Moreno	147	Aug. 13	at Atlanta	Byrd
125	May 21	at Chicago	Mitre	148	Aug. 14	at Atlanta	Ortiz
126	May 23	at Chicago	Clement	149	Aug. 14	at Atlanta	Ortiz
127	May 29	at Houston	Miller	150	Aug. 15	at Atlanta	Martin
128	May 29	at Houston	Miller	151	Aug. 16	Cincinnati	Riedling
129	May 30	at Houston	Backe	152	Aug. 21	Pittsburgh	Burnett
130	June 1	at Pittsburgh	Boehringer	153	Aug. 25	at Cincinnati	Hudson
131	June 2	at Pittsburgh	Wells	154	Aug. 29	at Pittsburgh	Meadows
132	June 18	Cincinnati	Matthews	155	Aug. 31	San Diego	Stone
133	June 19	Cincinnati	Acevedo	156	Sept. 1	San Diego	Linebrink
134	June 23	Chicago	Rusch	157	Sept. 2	San Diego	Peavy
135	July 3	Seattle	Franklin	158	Sept. 16	Houston	Backe
136	July 9	Chicago	Maddux	159	Sept. 24	at Colorado	Jennings
137	July 1	at Cincinnati	Sanchez	160	Sept. 26	at Colorado	Gissell

Career Multiple Home Run Games

Date	Opponent	No. of HR
April 22, 2001	at Houston	2
May 28, 2001	Milwaukee	2
April 30, 2003	New York (NL)	2
June 29, 2003	at Kansas City	2
Aug. 31, 2003	at Cincinnati	2
Sept. 10, 2003	Colorado	2
April 8, 2004	Milwaukee	2
May 29, 2004	at Houston	2
July 20, 2004	at Chicago	3
Aug. 14, 2004	at Atlanta	2

Career Postseason Home Runs

Date	Opponent	Pitcher	Round (Game)
Oct. 10, 2001	at Arizona	Johnson	Division (2)
Oct. 9, 2002	San Francisco	Rueter	NLCS (1)
Oct. 5, 2004	Los Angeles	Perez	Division (1)
Oct. 10, 2004	at Los Angeles	Alvarez	Division (4)
Oct. 13, 2004	Houston	Backe	NLCS (1)
Oct. 14, 2004	Houston	Miceli	NLCS (2)
Oct. 17, 2004	at Houston	Oswalt	NLCS (4)
Oct. 20, 2004	Houston	Munro	NLCS (6)

Career Milestones 2001-2004

Best Rookie Seasons of All Time

Player, Team	Year	Avg.	HR	RBI	Runs
Hal Trosky, Clev.	1934	.330	35	142	117
Ted Williams, Bos	1939	.327	31	145	131
Walt Dropo, Bos	1950	.322	34	144	101
Albert Pujols, Stl	2001	.329	37	130	112

Pursuit of Rookie Records

Category	Pujols 2001 Season	Previous NL Rookie Record
Batting Avg.	.329	.373, George Watkins, Stl, 1930
Runs	112	135, Roy Thomas, Phil, 1899
Hits	194	223, Lloyd Waner, Pitt, 1927
Total Bases	360	352, Dick Allen, Phil, 1964
Extra Base Hits	88	82, Johnny Frederick, Brkn, 1929
Doubles	47	52, Johnny Frederick, Brkn, 1929
Home Runs	37	38, Wally Berger, Bos, 1930 and Frank Robinson, Cin, 1956
RBI	130	119, Wally Berger, Bos, 1930

Most Home Runs, First Three Seasons

Player	Number
Ralph Kiner, Pitt, 1946-48	114
Albert Pujols, Stl, 2001-03	114
Eddie Mathews, Mil, 1952-54	112
Joe DiMaggio, NYY, 1936-38	107

Albert the Great: The Albert Pujols Story

Career Milestones 2001~2004

Youngest to 100 Home Runs

Player	Year	Age
Mel Ott	1931	22.132
Tony Conigliaro	1967	22.197
Eddie Mathews	1954	22.292
Alex Rodriguez	1998	23.016
Andruw Jones	2000	23.062
Johnny Bench	1971	23.161
Albert Pujols	2003	23.185
Hank Aaron	1957	23.191

Most RBI, First Four Major League Seasons

Player	Years	RBI
Joe DiMaggio	1936-39	558
Ted Williams	1939-42	515
Albert Pujols	2001-04	504

Career Bests, Single Game

Hits: 5, three times, most recent July 20, 2004 at Chicago
Runs: 4, July 20, 2004 at Chicago
Doubles: 2, 21 times, most recent Oct. 3, 2004 vs. Milwaukee
Home Runs: 3, July 20, 2004 at Chicago
RBI: 5, five times, most recent Aug. 16, 2004 vs. Cincinnati
Walks: 4, May 27, 2004 vs. Pittsburgh

Longest Hitting Streaks in Cardinals' History

Player	Year	Length
Rogers Hornsby	1922	33 games
Stan Musial	1950	30 games
Albert Pujols	2003	30 games
Harry Walker	1943	29 games
Ken Boyer	1959	29 games